Richard Rohr

and the

Enneagram Secret

Richard Rohr and the Enneagram Secret

Foreword by H. Wayne House

Don Veinot
Joy Veinot
Marcia Montenegro

Edited by Corkey McGehee

MCOI Publishing LLC
Wonder Lake, IL

©March 2020 by:
Don Veinot, Joy Veinot, and Marcia Montenegro

Published by:
MCOI Publishing LLC
Wonder Lake, IL 60097

Printed in the United States of America on FSC and SFI certified paper by:
BookBaby
Pennsauken, New Jersey 08110

Unless otherwise noted, all Scripture quotations are from the ESV® Bible (The Holy Bible, English Standard Version®) ©2001 by Crossway, a publishing ministry of Good News Publishers. Used by permission. All rights reserved.

Readers should be aware the internet websites offered as primary-source citations and/or other sources for further information may have changed or disappeared between the time this was written and when it is read. MCOI has many of the sources stored when they were accessed. Documentation provided upon written request.

ISBN 978-1-09830-654-0 (paperback)
ISBN 978-1-09830-655-7 (eBook)

Enneagram, Christian Apologetics, Occultism – Religious Aspects, New Age Movement, Evangelical Doctrine, Ritual Religious Practices, Christian Mysticism, Perennialism, Panentheism, Pantheism, Divination, Gnosticism

Cover, book design and layout: Sherwin (Todd) McGehee

Editing and proofreading: Donna (Corkey) McGehee

Dedications

I would like to dedicate my chapters to the late Dr. Norman Geisler and to Southern Evangelical Seminary. The Bible-based, sound theological teachings I received gave me the tools for not only understanding and appreciating Scripture, but also for evaluating whatever theologies and ideologies I might come across. I used those tools for my analysis of the topics of/in this book, and I am forever grateful to Dr. Geisler and my professors. Dr. Geisler's immense knowledge and his love for the Lord were contagious and all students like me benefited.

Marcia Montenegro
Founder,
Christian Answers for the New Age
www.christiananswersforthenewage.org

Working on a project such as this, we sometimes ask ourselves how church leaders—even those who once seemed so solid in their own teaching—can become so blind to error that they could permit such a widespread invasion of false teachings into the church? Additionally, how and why it is that individual Christians within these churches cannot see that teachings which are being presented are far removed from the "faith once for all delivered to the saints"?

We have a friend, associate, and member of our Advisory Board, Bill Honsberger, who occasionally makes it his mission to call and give me a simple four-word sentence as a reminder of why we do what we do. The sentence: "God loves the church." That's true. It is, in fact, *His* church. With that in mind, we dedicate this work to the Lord and to His church—the body of Christ. We pray our offering is useful to awaken His shepherds and protect His people.

L.L. (Don) and Joy A. Veinot,
Founders and President,
Midwest Christian Outreach, Inc.
www.midwestoutreach.org

Index of Illustrations

Contents

Editors Note:
All underlines found inside quotes are added by the authors for emphasis.

Foreword

I was encouraged when Don and Joy Veinot and Marcia Montenegro chose to tackle the unfortunate slide of many within the evangelical church into a fascination with an occult and New Age religious perspective and method known as the Enneagram. The announced intention of this psychological approach is to help Christians in personality development, Christian maturity, and spirituality. Several popular authors advocate this approach, but probably Richard Rohr has the most influence with the Christian church, even the evangelical wing.

Though this ideology makes a claim for legitimacy within the history of Christian thought, the evidence is non-existent. In fact, it comes from esoteric, Gnostic-like teachings. In order to support its themes and history to arrive at its conclusions, there is need for considerable imagination—even attempts to find connection with the Tower of Babel and ancient Egypt. Such, however, were it true, does not demonstrate that it flows from the historical revelation of God to the patriarchs, the people of Israel, the first-century church, or the orthodox, patristic community. The only basis of its connection to Christian history is that some of its ideas are akin to aspects of early Christian heresy of the second century and the unfortunate move, in some Roman Catholic communities in the Medieval period and today, towards an unbiblical and unhealthy mysticism. The focus is on looking within and following the nine-point symbol of the philosophy to become like the Christ.

Why would such a viewpoint be invited into the Christian church of today? The only reason that I can deduce is that the current commitment of many within the modern church is to post-modern and existential ideas and inner experience—views that fail to recognize the truth of Scripture—rather than the Scriptures which are able to build us to become like Jesus the Messiah. When the church neglects or rejects careful and systematic study of the Scriptures, people start looking for something else to solve their problems and yearnings. Unlike the writer Jude, who says that we are *"to contend for the faith that is once for all committed to the saints"* (Jude 1:3), many within the modern church have largely given lip service to the written revelation of God and the necessity to faithfully study the pages of Scripture with a historical and grammatical interpretative method. Rather, the Bible is proof-texted by many preachers to push for personal introspection based on "following one's heart." In addition, contemplative prayer and meditation has become a substitute for the blessed believer of Psalm 1 who *"meditates day and night"* (Psalm 1:2) in the instruction of God in the Word.

The teaching of the Enneagram is so far removed from the teaching of Scripture, that it becomes problematic to understand why evangelical publishing houses would even print these New Age books, unless they are just publishing what sells and not what follows Scripture and moves the Christian to be spiritually mature. Every major Christian doctrine regarding God, Jesus, salvation, and sanctification, et al, is denied, distorted, or assaulted by this occult religious teaching that attempts to robe itself in Christian dress. I commend Don and Joy Veinot and Marcia Montenegro for faithfully addressing and explaining this heretical departure from the Christian faith in the spirit of the Christian apologists of past centuries.

H. Wayne House, M.A., Th.D., J.D.
Distinguished Research Professor of Theology, Law, and Culture,
Faith International University and Faith Seminary

What Leaders are Saying

THE ENNEAGRAM IS DANGEROUS TO YOUR SPIRI-TUAL HEALTH! Want to know why? Read this eye-opening book. It's written by trustworthy apologists who are well-versed in the hidden dangers of the Enneagram. Highly recommended.

Dr. Ron Rhodes
Christian Apologist & Author

False ideas are one of the greatest obstacles to the Gospel and can lead even orthodox Christians astray. Most Christians can identify some of these false ideas: Marxism, Humanism, Evolution, and the New Age Movement. But few would be able to list the Enneagram as a false and dangerous idea. Richard Rohr, and those whom he has mentored, are spreading this idea. That is why this book is so important. It is a warning to Christians who might adopt it into their theology, and it is an obstacle to non-Christians who accept its teachings rather than the truth of the Gospel.

Kerby Anderson
President, Probe Ministries
Host, *Point of View* radio talk show

With meticulous research and sound biblical doctrine, Don and Joy Veinot and Marcia Montenegro show why we should avoid the Enneagram. *Richard Rohr and the Enneagram Secret* reveals the shockingly heretical underpinnings of the Enneagram, and how it has been deceptively marketed as an ancient Christian tool. This book is a must-read!

Doreen Virtue
Author, *Deceived No More*

Don and Joy Veinot and Marcia Montenegro have done the body of believers, indeed, their fellow human beings, a great service in researching and writing *Richard Rohr and the Enneagram Secret*. The growing enthusiasm about the Enneagram, both inside and outside the Christian church, might be dismissed as a trendy fad soon to fade away. But the toxicity of the occult background of the Enneagram and the heretical views of Richard Rohr require a swift, skillful, and thorough exposure and refutation. This they have done here. *Richard Rohr and the Enneagram Secret* should be read by everyone committed to sound Christian thinking; by those who want to keep others from falling prey to the Enneagram's false ideas; and by Christians who minister to those already deceived.

Richard G. Howe, Ph.D.
Emeritus Professor of Philosophy and Apologetics,
Southern Evangelical Seminary
Past President,
International Society of Christian Apologetics

Man looks at the outward appearance, but the Lord looks at your Enneagram, right? That's what many evangelical churches and institutions are advocating through their less-than-secret endorsement of this New Age paradigm of spirituality. The Enneagram is not a corporate, business self-assessment, or a means to discovering your personality type, or the *modus operandi* by which the Holy Spirit reveals your spiritual gifts. Rather, as Marcia Montenegro and Don and Joy Veinot chart in their well-researched work, the Enneagram is a New Age, mystical, path to God. Each of the nine points or personality types allegedly indicates specific paths to God and the face of God, Himself. To claim there are any other paths to God apart from the person and work of Jesus Christ flies in the very face of Scripture and the Gospel itself. We owe a great debt to Montenegro and the Veinots for their well-researched, robust, response to this New Age form of heresy that has crept into the church. *Tolle lege!*

William C. Roach, Ph.D.
President,
International Society of Christian Apologetics

One would not have thought that discernment in the evangelical world could still reach a new low. One would be wrong. With mainstream evangelical publishers like Zondervan and InterVarsity Press promoting books on the Enneagram, the final proof that much of the "evangelical" publishing industry is only about money, not truth, is now inescapable.

The Enneagram is a geometric figure, a circle containing nine points, being pushed as a tool for personality typing and finding one's path to God. Widely believed to be of ancient origin, its roots are actually in modern occultism and New-Age spirituality. It is utterly devoid of any scientific psychological basis or biblical content. Don and Joy Veinot and Marcia Montenegro expose the facts in a book that should never have been necessary—but it is. In *Richard Rohr and the Enneagram Secret,* they leave no stone unturned in revealing the true source, nature, and danger of this hoax. Well-researched and clearly written, the book is a must-read for anyone who wants to be up on the latest trends in cult research, anyone wondering if the Enneagram has any validity, or anyone who knows someone influenced by it.

Donald T. Williams, Ph.D.
R. A. Forrest Scholar & Prof. of English,
Toccoa Falls College
Past President,
International Society of Christian Apologetics

If you don't know anything about the Enneagram or you want to know its relationship to Christianity, this book has much to offer. Montenegro and the Veinots, experts in the material, take the reader through the primary resources on the Enneagram and compare its teachings to Scripture and orthodox Christian teaching in order to show that the Enneagram is anything but Christian. With the rise in popularity of the Enneagram in evangelical circles, this is a book you need to read!

J. Brian Huffling, Ph.D.
Director of Ph.D. Program
Associate Professor of Philosophy and Theology,
Southern Evangelical Seminary, Charlotte, NC

In Matthew 24, Jesus warns multiple times that believers should be on their guard for deception, particularly in the last days. The Apostle Paul also warns in 2 Timothy 4, in very stark terms, that deception will abound in the latter days:

> *For the time will come when they will not endure sound doctrine; but after their own lusts shall they heap to themselves teachers, having itching ears; And they shall turn away their ears from the truth, and shall be turned unto fables.* (2 Timothy 4:3-4, KJV)

For many years, modern evangelicalism has quickly adapted to a series of fads that are, without question, based on false teaching, and which incorporate pagan, mystical and New Age practices into the church. In other words, the leaders of the latest fad are fulfilling that about which the Apostle Paul warned.

In observing the state of modern evangelicalism, I know of no fad that has swept across the evangelical landscape as quickly as the Enneagram. Hardly a day passes without learning of a formerly sound church, a college, or a seminary that has turned to the fable of the Enneagram.

This new book, *Richard Rohr and the Enneagram Secret*, is a masterful work that dismantles how the Enneagram developed and how it came to be introduced into the church. It is imperative that pastors and those in charge of seminaries and colleges learn the truth of this myth. You cannot read this book and come to any other conclusion that massive deception is at play.

I am grateful that Don & Joy Veinot and Marcia Montenegro have blessed the church with this research. Please read it and act accordingly and get it out of your church, your college or your seminary if the leadership does not respond to the information and address the false teaching. Don't. Fall. For. It.

John Haller
Elder and Teacher,
Fellowship Bible Chapel in Sunbury, OH
Host, *John Haller's Prophecy Update* (YouTube)

The authors provide exhaustive documentation based on a thorough investigation of the claims and sources of the Enneagram. Their analysis of the many unbiblical, theological teachings of Enneagram authors makes it abundantly clear that the Enneagram system is antithetical to biblical Christianity. They ask important questions about how the Enneagram could find its way into evangelical churches, institutions, and publishing houses. I particularly appreciate their debunking of panentheism and its errors and dangers. The authors provide a timely call for Christians to return to sound doctrine and develop a biblical worldview. I heartily endorse this book.

Bob DeWaay
Theologian and teacher,
Gospel of Grace Fellowship, Edina, MN
Author, *Critical Issues Commentary*

The Christian worldview can be undermined unless each and every thought is brought captive to Christ. Ideas that put anything, including ourselves, at the center rather than Jesus as king *must* be rejected. The same goes for the church. The authors expose an old heretical idea which is now dressed up as a harmless tool of self-analysis. They warn us that we cannot blithely welcome this idea because ideas come wrapped in worldviews. They trace the origins and weigh the implications of the Enneagram and demonstrate it is not only distracting for the church but dangerous to the faith once delivered to the saints. Let those who have an ear to hear take heed their admonitions and consider their warnings.

Jonathan Miles, Ph.D.
Associate Professor of Philosophy,
Quincy University, Quincy, IL

Another spiritual trend has entered the church, another technique for Self-empowerment, another promised path to enlightenment. Unpacking the history and meaning of the Enneagram, Don and Joy Veinot and Marcia Montenegro effectively demonstrate that this is another search for truth in the wrong place.

Carl Teichrib
Author,
Game of Gods:
The Temple of Man in the Age of Re-Enchantment

Occult inroads into modern medicine are legion and are typically under-exposed. But now we see the inroads of the unexamined into evangelical institutions that sadly and too frequently lack basic, worldview discernment. This book can help the teachable do significantly better. Those enraptured by any new tool to use to talk about themselves/ourselves likely initially will be resistive. Can we read and reason outside our psychology-sharing clique? If one can do so, they will find help to recover genuine care for people while upholding a biblical view of the image of God in humanity without the unexamined, default endorsement of every ostensibly, spiritual resource. Reading this book can help one to grow in discernment. Thanks for this needed exposé.

Joe B. Whitchurch
Vice President, Campus Operations,
Ratio Christi

You need to read this book! I first became aware of the Ennea-gram in the 1980s when it became a passing fad in New Age and metaphysical bookstores across the country. As the novelty wore off, the Enneagram's popularity waned, and it seemed to be fading into obscurity. Inexplicably, some 40-years later, major evangelical Christian publishers have resurrected the Enneagram and attempted to baptize it as some kind of biblical resource or Christian tool. A new generation of Christians is now vulnerable to spiritual dangers, because they are completely unaware of the Enneagram's modern origins and its underlying occult principles.

James Walker
President,
Watchman Fellowship
Co-founder,
The Atheist & Christian Book Club

I have been concerned for some time about the growing influ-ence of the New Age Movement on Christians. *Richard Rohr and the Enneagram Secret* offers a thought-provoking perspective on one conduit of this influence by providing compelling evidence of New Age philosophy within the Enneagram. Don and Joy Veinot and Marcia Montenegro clearly identify these New Age beliefs in ever-increasingly-popular, Christian books that erroneously present the Enneagram as a means of self-awareness and spiritual growth. I recommend *Richard Rohr and the Enneagram Secret* as essential reading for anyone in Christian leadership.

Danny Loe
Director of International Missions,
Ratio Christi

The "Enneagram of Personality," promoted by some Christian publishers, is now being heralded from church pulpits and studied in small groups. And yet, this latest craze does not have its origin in either the Bible or church history, but in the occult and spiritu-alism. The authors, Don and Joy Veinot and Marcia Montenegro, help those interested to assess this phenomenon by uncovering its history in detail and also its non-Christian world view and elements.

Dr. James Bjornstad
Professor of Philosophy (retired),
Cedarville University

Christians everywhere are excited about the Enneagram. It's difficult to miss the waves it has been making in the church over the last three years, and its proponents are extremely vocal and not in any way open to criticism. With clarity and precision, this book will walk you through what the Enneagram actually is, and why Christians should tear down this idol and remove it from the church as quickly as possible.

Summer White
Blogger and Co-Host,
Sheologians Podcast

Appreciations

The three of us appreciate those who have gone before us in defense of the faith in both the recent and distant past. Some of God's people who were standing firm and preserving God's truth appear in the pages of holy writ, and their deeds are stamped indelibly in the minds of those who, like us, have to spend time ferreting out and addressing false teaching among God's people when we would far prefer to be addressing the unbiblical teachings of cults and false religions. Closer to our day, we appreciate the work of J. Gresham Machen whose 1923 book, *Christianity & Liberalism*, addressed the liberal Christianity making such headway in his day and laid out the stark differences between true Christianity and Christianity in name only. We also appreciate the work of those apologists whom we have had the privilege of knowing personally, such as Dr. Norman Geisler (Co-founder and President of Southern Evangelical Seminary and author/co-author of over 100 books), who took a firm stand in defense of the faith. Dr. Geisler, although personally a gentle man and an example of a true servant who recently went home to be with the Lord, was completely undeterred and forthright in his defense of the historic Christian faith and his stand against biblical error. He taught us to focus on addressing the facts of issues rather than attacking persons with whom we may disagree. He was friend to the three of us (Don, Joy, Marcia); and he was an always-accessible mentor who was ever ready with either a joke or serious answer to a tough question. Dr. Ron Rhodes (Founder and President of Reasoning from the Scriptures Ministry and author of over 60 books), another friend and mentor, conveyed to us the value of reading two good books for every bad book one must read to carry on apologetics research. These individuals and so many more were wise in their advice to check sources, to quote them in context, and to respond accurately.

There was also quite a team actively involved in this project who deserve more than acknowledgment but a very public thank you of appreciation! Dr. Ronald V. Huggins [B.F.A., Th.D., formerly of Moody Bible Institute (Spokane), Salt Lake Theological Seminary, and Midwestern Baptist Theological Seminary] tirelessly searched out details of ancient history, the Post-Nicene and Desert Fathers, as well as some of the key twentieth-century players. His willingness to read the draft and offer suggestions was of immense value.

Roger Corbin (studies in church history at Gordon Conwell Theological Seminary) is another friend who spent a great deal of time, as we did, trying to persuade publishers of Enneagram books and materials to take a serious look into the factual history of the Enneagram. One publisher responded back to written correspondence by simply parroting the Enneagram is ancient. We contacted another publisher and their parent company, but neither responded. Although they were unwilling to heed our concerns, in our estimation, it was worth the effort to try to educate them. Roger also spent time and energy tracking down sources, primary source quotes, and information as well as reading and critiquing the draft as we went.

Pastor Dan Cox from Wonder Lake Bible Church spent his precious time reading and critiquing the draft. He also faithfully prayed for the three of us as we worked together researching and assembling the material to create what we hope is an understandable treatment of the Enneagram issues. Coming into the project with little knowledge of the Enneagram and reading it as a shepherd who takes his mandate of guarding the flock seriously, he also pressed us to write with clarity for those who may know little to nothing about the Enneagram, so they could absorb and understand the seriousness of the issue. Dan is more than our pastor; he is also our friend and fellow traveler along this road of faith.

In addition to others who read the draft, there are two whom we owe special appreciation: Todd and Corkey McGehee. They have been working behind the scenes with the ministry of Midwest Christian Outreach, Inc. since 1994. Todd has been ever faithful in graphic design, layout, and making our printed works look professional. Corkey, his wife, is our Senior Editor and proofreader, and she approaches every project as through the eyes of someone who knows little to nothing about the subject or the Bible. She spends hours reading, checking, fixing, and offering suggestions—all which serve to improve the end result and hold us accountable to the Lord and His people on the printed page. Since 1994, they have prayed for us, challenged us, and been there for us in so many other ways.

To all of these and so many more, we say, "Thank you!"

CHAPTER 1

Enneagram 101: The Road Map

Why is it that you have this particular book? Is it because, even though you have never heard of the Enneagram (pronounced like any-a-gram), the title and cover caught your interest? Perhaps you have heard the term from friends or family who have become involved with it, but you know very little and are looking for information. Possibly your church or a church you know of has introduced it to their congregation. They assumed it is a personality profile of sorts or a spiritual tool designed to bring someone closer to God. It is all the rage in certain segments of the church; but you have never really heard of it before. For those who are just beginning investigation, we are starting with basic information—a sort of Enneagram 101 with particular points of interest like markers on a road map.

The starting point is the Enneagram itself. It is a geometric design consisting of a circle with an equilateral triangle and an irregular hexagram inside which touch the circle at nine points. The current version has numbers added at the touch points around the circle as can be seen in the following diagram.

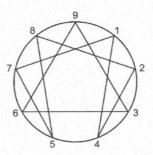

Current Version of the Enneagram

At the moment, it does seem to be all the rage; but prior to 2016, very few within the evangelical and confessing church had even heard of the Enneagram. There is a reason this is the case. Since its inception, it only resided within the domain of the occult, New Age, and a handful of Roman Catholic priests. While it is true most of the writers, promoters, and teachers presently refer to this as the Enneagram of Personality, they also define what the term means, and what it does not mean. One of the more popular authors, Christopher L. Heuertz, quotes one of his teachers, New Ager and co-founder of the Enneagram Institute, Russ Hudson, who clarified:

Type isn't a 'type' of person, but a path to God.[1]

Each number within the Enneagram is "a path;" and with the help of Enneagram coaches and authors, it is up to the individual to discover which is their personal path. Do these paths lead to God or to somewhere else? The title of Ian Morgan Cron and Suzanne Stabile's popular book is *The Road Back to You: An Enneagram Journey to Self-Discovery*.[2] Likewise, Christopher L. Heuertz's best seller, *The Sacred Enneagram: Finding Your Unique Path to Spiritual Growth*,[3] puts the reader on a path to oneself. Is that the best place to find answers? A brief look at one short passage from just one of God's prophets provides a contrast:

> *Thus says the LORD: "Cursed is the man who trusts in man and makes flesh his strength, whose heart turns away from the LORD. He is like a shrub in the desert, and shall not see any good come. He shall dwell in the parched places of the*

wilderness, in an uninhabited salt land.
    "Blessed is the man who trusts in the LORD, whose trust is the LORD. He is like a tree planted by water, that sends out its roots by the stream, and does not fear when heat comes, for its leaves remain green, and is not anxious in the year of drought, for it does not cease to bear fruit.
    "The heart is deceitful above all things, and desperately sick; who can understand it?" (Jeremiah 17:5-10)

There are two spiritual guides compared and contrasted this passage. One whose focus and trust is in him or herself:

    Cursed is the man who trusts in man and makes flesh his strength.

The other whose focus is on God. The LORD also describes how the first took a wrong turn:

    The heart is deceitful above all things, and desperately sick; who can understand it?

As we read through the books, literature, and teachings by the "Enneagram masters," coaches, and guides and compare them with Scripture, we find they hold unbiblical views regarding the human condition, God, and salvation.

In an effort to establish the Enneagram as a valid tool, the current popular authors claim the Enneagram is very ancient, used in a number of cultures, civilizations, and religions since near the earliest times in recorded human history. In their claims about history, they include some of the church's "Desert Fathers."[4] We will briefly touch on this with a few road markers in this chapter. We will observe the spiritual landscape at greater depth in the following chapters as we explore the claims, evidence, and where the teachings, lead.

We believe many in church leadership who have integrated the Enneagram into their church and introduced it to those who attend their churches have done so with the best of intentions. It is being marketed by mainstream evangelical publishers and promoted by high-profile evangelical leaders. However, pastors and church leadership are charged with guarding the flock (Acts 20:28-20). We must ask: Have they done their due diligence?

Basic Facts[5]

The following is a brief, seventeen-point overview of the history, claims, and known facts about the Enneagram:

1. Fictional claim: The Enneagram is ancient, going back to the Desert Fathers, Evagrius Ponticus, or Ramón Llull.
The claim is false. The Enneagram originated with esoteric teacher **GEORGE I. GURDJIEFF**[6] (1866?-1949) Scholars have verified this, and we will look at this more in-depth in chapter 4.
2. Fictional claim: Gurdjieff's followers claimed he got the Enneagram from a secret Sufi brotherhood.
This is a false claim: This was not factually supported originally and was later debunked.

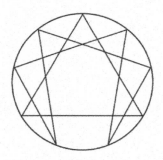

The Original Enneagram by George I. Gurdjieff

3. George Gurdjieff's original Enneagram had no numbers or "types" (see image above) and had nothing whatsoever to do with personality. According to Gurdjieff, it was a diagram of "cosmic reality." He believed one could see the universe in it, and he ascribed mystical meaning to it.
4. Gurdjieff's pupil, **P.D. OUSPENSKY** (1878-1947), wrote about Gurdjieff's ideas and called those teachings "The Fourth Way." (These beliefs influenced the New Age).

5. Gurdjieff's teachings were adopted by **OSCAR ICHAZO** (1931-2020) who ran an occult school in Arica, Chile (founded 1968). He added various ideas to the Enneagram, but he did not use it for personality typing. It should be known that Ichazo had contact with two spirits—Metatron and the Green Q'tub.[7]

6. **CLAUDIO NARANJO** (1932-2019), a New Age psychiatrist and spiritual seeker, learned about the Enneagram from Ichazo. Naranjo claimed to add the personality types partly from his "observations" but "mostly" via automatic writing. (He makes these claim on video.[8])

7. Fiction acknowledged: Naranjo stated that he and Ichazo fabricated the idea that the Enneagram was ancient, and he admits it was not. He pointed to Oscar Wilde as justification. Naranjo claimed Wilde said, "If you want your idea to become famous, attribute it to a famous person."[9]

8. Naranjo took the Enneagram ideas to **ESALEN** (founded 1962), an edgy, humanistic/New Age think tank in Big Sur, California in the 1960s. Esalen is characterized by Dr. Ronald V. Huggins, formerly of Moody Bible Institute (Spokane), Salt Lake Theological Seminary, and Midwestern Baptist Theological Seminary, as "a place where people were likely to get naked, take LSD, and beat on native drums." (See note chapter 4, note 24.)

9. The Enneagram was introduced into the New Age from Esalen as were other New Age ideas. The Enneagram became big business in the New Age starting in the 1980s. New Agers, New Age psychotherapists, and psychics began giving interpretations to the "types" initially with the idea that the Enneagram uncovers a true "divine self." One of the main New Age psychic/intuitive writers and teachers is Helen Palmer.

10. Roman Catholic Jesuit Priest Bob Ochs (1930-2018) was at Esalen and learned the Enneagram from Naranjo. In turn, Ochs introduced it into the Roman Catholic Church where it mainly spread to New Age thinking priests. (The Roman Catholic Church never endorsed it.)

11. **RICHARD ROHR** (1943-), who learned the Enneagram as a Catholic priest, wrote a book on it in the early 1990s. Richard Rohr mentions that Helen Palmer became involved with the Enneagram because, being a psychic/intuitive, she believes she can train people to be psychic/intuitive. Richard Rohr states, "that's what

this was about initially. I mean, we didn't use that kind of word in the early centuries."[10]

12. In 1992, another Roman Catholic Jesuit Priest, **MITCH PACWA** (1949-), wrote the book *Catholics and the New Age: How Good People are Being Drawn into Jungian Psychology, the Enneagram, and the Age of Aquarius* to warn Roman Catholics about the heresy which was being promoted.

13. In the beginning of the twenty-first century, as Emergent and Progressive Christianity grew, Richard Rohr's influence on the Emergent/Progressive Movement sparked interest in the Enneagram as the next step after Contemplative Prayer.[11] The Enneagram was presented at their churches and conferences.

14. In the Fall 1991 issue, the Christian Research Institute published an article in their *CRI Journal* by Fr. Mitch Pacwa, SJ, "Tell Me Who I Am, O Enneagram," in an attempt to warn evangelicals of the origins and occult nature of the Enneagram.[12]

15. In March of 2011, Christian researcher and former New Ager/Astrologer Marcia Montenegro posted an article, "The Enneagram GPS: Gnostic Path to Self" on her Christian Answers for the New Age website (http://www.christiananswersforthenewage. org) as a warning to evangelicals.[13]

16. The Enneagram's popularity led to two books on the Enneagram, both of which are now widely used in the church. Both books were written by students and followers of Rohr. Episcopal Priest and psychotherapist **IAN CRON** (1960-) with co-author **SUZANNE STABILE** (1954-), who was mentored by Rohr for many years, wrote *The Road Back to You* (IVP, 2016). **CHRISTOPHER HEUERTZ** (1971-) wrote the book entitled *The Sacred Enneagram* (Zondervan, 2017). Richard Rohr wrote the foreword of this book, and Heuertz thanks his Enneagram teachers: Richard Rohr and three New Agers.

17. One cannot disconnect the Enneagram from Richard Rohr, which is why it is essential to know his beliefs, especially since the writers of the two main books in use among evangelicals are his students and have taught at his Center for Action and Contemplation (CAC). One needs to know that Rohr denies the biblical doctrines on man, sin, creation, salvation, and God. Richard Rohr also teaches a false Jesus/Christ. Rohr makes a distinction between Jesus and Christ by saying Jesus was not the "Universal Christ" who is

"bigger" than Jesus. To Richard Rohr, the *creation is* Christ.

In summary, the origins of the Enneagram are in mysticism, occultism, and New Age. It has no origins in history prior to the early twentieth century. In fact, it is not based on empirically validated psychological theories or psychometric studies. It is based on the intuitive and occult-based mystical experiences of one man: Claudio Naranjo.

The Enneagram is no more valid than Astrology and, as we shall see, may be more dangerous. If validation for the Enneagram is based on how people are "helped," it should be noted that many more people believe in Astrology as describing, guiding, and helping them; but their belief does not make it valid, true, or *actually* useful. *Belief* in something or thinking something "works" validates nothing. The claims about the Enneagram crumble once the facts are known.

Unfortunately, pastors, ministry leaders, counselors, and others are either relying on false information or on others who, themselves, are relying on false information concerning the Enneagram. As belief in and use of the Enneagram spreads, the myths upon which it is based continue to go largely unchallenged. The content and resources provided in this book are for those who desire to know the origins and history of the Enneagram including the worldviews, spiritual beliefs, and claims of its originators and architects. Equipped with this information, readers will be better prepared to guard themselves and others against deception. It is our prayer that our Lord Jesus Christ uses it to that end.

CHAPTER 2

Forbidden Fruit

*N*ow the serpent was more crafty than any other beast of
the field that the LORD God had made. (Genesis 3:1)

The book of Genesis gives us the explanation of origins. From
where did the cosmos and all that exists come? With no fanfare or
elucidation, the book opens with four words: *"In the beginning,
God"* (Genesis 1:1). The Creation account culminates in chapter 2
with two human beings who were created in God's image—Adam
and Eve—as the beginning of the human race. They were living in
what truly was a garden paradise. It was filled with all sorts of creatures which God had created. There was plant life in abundance
and much of it edible. God and all His creation was theirs to enjoy
with one caveat: There was a tree in the midst of the garden which
they were free to enjoy as part of the landscape, but they could not
partake of the fruit of that *one* tree. That was forbidden. The passage
ends with a simple statement:

> And the man and his wife were both naked and were not
> ashamed. (Genesis 2:25)

To use a common idiom, they were "comfortable in their own skin." Paraphrasing the *Free Dictionary*, "they had a relaxed confidence in and clear understanding of themselves, their abilities."[1] They enjoyed vast freedom. They were free from distrust, doubt, and the feeling something was missing. They had but one limitation: they must not eat of the tree in the midst of the garden. What happened next would change all of that for themselves and all their descendants, which includes you and me.

We now observe the origins of deception unfold. A false teacher showed up—the serpent of old; and with a few subtly deceptive questions, Eve was deceived. What he offered was but a slightly nuanced change in Gods words; but from that misrepresentation sprang all the evils of this world.

> He said to the woman, "Did God actually say, 'You shall not eat of any tree in the garden?'" And the woman said to the serpent, "We may eat of the fruit of the trees in the garden, but God said, 'You shall not eat of the fruit of the tree that is in the midst of the garden, neither shall you touch it, lest you die.'" (Genesis 3:1b-3:3)

The *Faithlife Study Bible* points out:

> The serpent's question omits the positive statement made by God in Genesis 2:16 where the man is told *"You may surely eat of every tree of the garden."* The serpent also distorts the earlier statement by presenting God as saying Adam and Eve could not eat from any tree at all.[2]

Even though Eve corrected the serpent, a curiosity was aroused in her by her deceitful opponent which would have profound effects. The wedge had been put in place, and it was all that was needed was for the false teacher to drive it in to split the relationship between God and Adam and Eve. The tempter did it by a simple process. First, he cast doubt on the word of God. Second, he cast doubt on the character of God.

> *You will not surely die.* (Genesis 3:4b)

The "crafty" serpent told Eve straight out that she could not really believe *everything* God had said. The serpent implied God may have had ulterior motives in withholding this particular fruit. The serpent led her down the path to wondering if God was keeping something from her which would rob her of knowledge that would help her reach her full potential. Perhaps He would deprive her of realizing her "true self."[3]

> *For God knows that when you eat of it your eyes will be opened, and you will be like God, knowing good and evil.* (Genesis 3:5)

She could be like God! Was God holding back something of great importance from them? Was God really good after all, or was He selfishly holding them back? Perhaps she and Adam could be on an equal footing with God! Her attention was, thus, turned away from all the wonderful gifts God had given them and was focused on the forbidden fruit. The next verse tells us what happened:

> *So when the woman saw that the tree was good for food, and that it was a delight to the eyes, and that the tree was to be desired to make one wise, she took of its fruit and ate, and she also gave some to her husband who was with her, and he ate.* (Genesis 3:6)

The Hebrew word translated *saw* means more than just viewing. It has the idea of *observing, examining, getting acquainted.*[4] Eve was intrigued and she touched the tree with seemingly no ill effect at all! The serpent had promised her she could attain Godlike wisdom and thus become all she could be. Though false, his promise seemed to be far more than God had offered her, and she took a bite. Adam was with her (Genesis 2:6), and he took and ate what Eve gave him. Too late came the realization of what they had brought upon themselves: Great fear and guilt set in, and they hid themselves from God. God had previously issued a warning they would surely die if they ate the fruit (Genesis 2:17); and while they had no experience with the horrors of death, it began to dawn on them that it was something very dreadful, indeed. The word *death* simply means *separation.*[5] One of the consequences of this separation from God was a devastating change that has dogged human beings ever since then: The focus changed from being on God and His creation on to oneself.

I Can Fix This

With this new self-focus, they were no longer comfortable in their own skin and attempted to remedy the situation on their own. Having turned away from God and His Word, they became engaged in fixing themselves. The first step they took is what we might call the great cover-up:

> *they sewed fig leaves together and made themselves loin-cloths.* (Genesis 3:7)

In addition to partially concealing themselves from one another, it seems they began to view God as a limited being with limited knowledge. That led them to part two of their fix. They began hiding from God:

> *And they heard the sound of the LORD God walking in the garden in the cool of the day, and the man and his wife hid themselves from the presence of the LORD God among the trees of the garden.* (Genesis 3:8)

That's the ticket. Blend in with the landscape! There was a slight problem with this particular fix. As it turns out, God is omniscient. That is, He is by nature all-knowing. Someone might ask, "If He is all-knowing, why did God call, *'Where are you?'*" (Genesis 3:9). Actually, it wasn't a question God needed to have answered. He already knew where Adam was, and what Adam and Eve had done. The question was for Adam's benefit. *The Apologetics Study Bible* comments:

> The Bible is full of affirmations of God's unlimited knowledge (see Ge 16:13; Ex 3:7; Job 12:13; 28:23-24; 36:4; Ps 33:13-15; 139:1-4; Is 46:10; Jr 23:24; Mt 10:29; Acts 15:8; Heb 4:13). Therefore God's questions here are rhetorical; He is not unaware of the couple's location and what had transpired in the garden. The passage describes God as a parent who instructs His children with restoration as His purpose.[6]

God already had the plan of redemption and restoration in mind; but like a good parent, He gave Adam the opportunity to come clean. What did Adam do when asked if he had eaten the forbidden fruit? Without a moment's hesitation, he asserted victim status! It was the fault of the woman God gave him, ultimately making it God's fault:

> *The woman whom you gave to be with me, she gave me fruit of the tree, and I ate.* (Genesis 3:12)

God's Provision

There were consequences to all of this. The serpent was cursed; no redemption was offered to him at all. Concerning his personal future destiny, the serpent was given a prophecy of his ultimate defeat and utter destruction by one of Eve's descendants—the coming Messiah (Genesis 3:15). This is referred to as the *protoevangelium* or *the first declaration of the Gospel.*[7]

Adam and Eve were banished from the garden. Eve was now destined to endure pain in childbearing. The formerly harmonious husband-wife relationship would now have stress in it which hadn't existed prior to the Fall. Adam was sentenced to hard, physical labor and was informed that nature and the elements would be against him. Their food would be whatever he was able to grow and harvest through adversity. On top of these things, they now had begun the process of physical death:

> *till you return to the ground, for out of it you were taken; for you are dust, and to dust you shall return.* (Genesis 3:19)

God demonstrated the principal that *"without the shedding of blood, there is no forgiveness of sins"* (Hebrews 9:22). God also communicates in Leviticus 17:11 *"the life of the flesh is in the blood, and I have given it for you on the altar to make atonement for your souls, for it is the blood that makes atonement by the life."* He provided the means to mend their severed relationship with Him by substituting sacrificial animals to die in their place. He then properly clothed them with these *"garments of skins"* which He had secured from the sacrifice, and which He personally had crafted for them (cf. Genesis 3:21). These garments would not only be a covering for Adam and Eve, but also continual reminders of the consequences (separation from God, death) and remedy (shed blood) for their sin. The proper relationship between God and humankind should be focused on God and living according to His word. Even today, our lives become infinitely more complicated and crooked when we lose focus on God, either by becoming focused on or deceiving ourselves, or by coming "under the spell" of false teachers and deceivers.

God in My Image

As we read through Scripture, we see some common themes: God reveals Himself and reaches out to mankind. After a time, however, human beings become focused on themselves yet again. They measure one another and God by an inflated view of themselves and create images of a limited god they can control and use for their own purposes. In their hubris, they create imaginative and self-aggrandizing new paths to God, rather than follow the path which God laid out for them. We human beings would rather be our own god than bow to the true God. It is a "heart condition" with which we are born as Adam and Eve's offspring. God spoke about this after the Flood:

> *I will never again curse the ground because of man, for the intention of man's heart is evil from his youth.* (Genesis 8:21)

This self-exaltation of human beings or their "heart condition" shows up with their construction of the Tower of Babel in Genesis 11. It is chronicled in the repeated rebellion against God in the history of the Nation of Israel as they adopted pagan gods, worship, and rituals. They didn't overtly reject God, but instead, they added into the mix other gods—ones that were more controllable and visible. Of course, God makes it clear that He views the incorporation of the worship of any other alleged deities into the worship of the one true God as spiritual adultery (cf. Jeremiah 3:8, 13:27). Herein lies a core problem. We can, and deceivers do, often deny God *implicitly* without doing so *explicitly*. Employing the cunning of the serpent in the garden, they may subtly suggest a slight alteration to "what God said" that doesn't unduly upset his or her target audience ... until they have been separated from God ... and they don't even realize it! But little-by-little, brick-by-brick, the false teacher turns the truth of God upside down. The late Carl Sagan repeatedly did this during his opening introduction to every episode of his television show *Cosmos*[8]:

> The Cosmos is all that is, or was, or ever will be. (Carl Sagan, *Cosmos* series, 1978-79)

What is he saying? It's simple: "There is no God." It isn't overt. If he opened up with, "There is no God" he may very well have lost a fair number of viewers. The universe is, indeed, glorious. It is vast. Scripture even tells us:

> *The heavens declare the glory of God, and the sky above proclaims his handiwork. Day to day pours out speech, and night to night reveals knowledge. There is no speech, nor are there words, whose voice is not heard. Their voice goes out through all the earth, and their words to the end of the world. In them he has set a tent for the sun, which comes out like a bridegroom leaving his chamber, and, like a strong man, runs its course with joy. Its rising is from the end of the heavens, and its circuit to the end of them, and there is nothing hidden from its heat.* (Psalm 19:1-6)

Sagan pointed to the universe—the Cosmos. The Psalmist points *past* the cosmos to the One Who created the cosmos. Sagan *implicitly* denied the Creator and, instead, worshiped the creation. We even see it became his God-substitute by always writing the word out with a capital "C"—Cosmos!

Testing Teachers

In a continuation of His teaching to the crowd at Matthew 5:1, Jesus warns the crowds in Matthew 7:15-23 to:

> *Beware of false prophets, who come to you in sheep's
> clothing but inwardly are ravenous wolves. You will recognize
> them by their fruits.* (Matthew 7:15-16)

In this passage, the fruits of false prophets are not their works; it is their works that will make them look like sheep. Rather, the fruits of false prophets are their *prophecies,* their claims, and their *teachings* in essential areas of the faith. We will not necessarily recognize false prophets/teachers by their good or "spiritual" appearance, because they will seem to be wearing sheep's clothing; *they will look like sheep!* Even today, pseudo-Christian groups like Jehovah's Witnesses, Mormons, and others appeal to their "good works" as the evidence proving they are God's one true group. By outward observation of their "works" (i.e., how they live), it appears they are Christian, but their prophecies, claims, and teachings in core areas of the biblical, Christian faith are false. The futility of the false prophets and false teachers appealing to external works as validation is even more clearly affirmed at the end of the Lord's warning when He said:

> *On that day many will say to me, 'Lord, Lord, did we not
> prophesy in your name, and cast out demons in your name,
> and do many mighty works in your name?' And then will I de-
> clare to them, 'I never knew you; depart from me, you workers
> of lawlessness.'* (Matthew 7:22-23)

The false prophets and teachers appealed to what they did (their outward works) and were rejected. The Jewish crowd listening to Jesus immediately would have thought back to the criteria for false prophets and false teachers given to them by Moses in Deuteronomy. In Deuteronomy 13, the entire chapter is devoted to those who claim to represent God—prophets and dreamers of dreams who may perform miracles, but who deceive you on the true nature of God. They are false prophets. It doesn't stop there though. Moses's condemnation included friends and family members who would mislead the people.

It is written in Deuteronomy 18:20-22 that if a prophet made predictions, claimed these "prophecies" came from the LORD, and these prophecies failed to come to pass, the self-proclaimed prophet was, in truth, a *false prophet* and was to be stoned to death. Maintaining a clear understanding on the essentials of the faith that had been revealed up until that time was of paramount importance. The truth from God was not to be changed or modified in any way. Therefore, those claiming to be speaking for the LORD had to be put to the test He gave to the people. As God continued His revelation to mankind, more criteria was revealed in response to false teachers and deceivers. Are those who are claiming to be prophets and teachers today honest with history? Do they faithfully adhere to the essentials of the faith as revealed in the Old and New Testaments? How do they stack up to biblical truth in their teachings regarding:

- the nature of God,
- the nature of Man,
- the nature of Sin,
- the nature of the Resurrection,
- the nature of Salvation,
- the inspiration and inerrancy of Scripture

As we study Scripture and correctly determine God's revelation of Himself, we find God is described as one true God, uncreated, Who exists eternally. God is all-knowing (omniscient), all-powerful (omnipotent), and everywhere present (omnipresent). He created everything that is created, but He is not part of or in the creation. Creation is entirely God's work, but it is not an extension of God's being. The one true God exists as three persons Who are co-equal, co-eternal, and co-powerful. We see the tri-unity of God's nature in the area of Creation. For example, in Genesis 1:1 we are told simply, *"In the beginning, God [plural noun] created [singular verb] the heavens and the earth."* However, 1 Corinthians 8:6 states, *"there is one God, the Father, from whom are all things and for whom we exist, and one Lord, Jesus Christ, through whom are all things and through whom we exist."* The one true God is the Father, and He is the Creator. Furthermore, John 1:1-3 informs the reader that the Son (*"the Word"*) is the Creator, adding that *"All things were made through him, and without him was not any thing made that was made."* In other words, if the Son did not create something, it is not created! Job 33:4 tells of the Holy Spirit being credited with

Creation: *"The Spirit of God has made me, and the breath of the Almighty gives me life."*

When we look at the nature of human beings, we find they were created by God. Humans were initially innocent, but they rebelled in the garden. Since then, the human condition is evil by nature. As the LORD said in Genesis 6:5, *"the intention of man's heart is evil from his youth."* In the New Testament, the Apostle Paul makes it abundantly clear in the first few chapters of Romans that man's true nature—man's "true self"—is corrupt. The sad state of mankind, as he writes in Romans 3:10-18, is that *"no one is righteous"* or seeks God and:

> *all have sinned and fall short of the glory of God.* (Romans 3:23)

Salvation or redemption is secured completely through God's grace—His *unmerited* kindness—by means of the death, burial, and physical Resurrection of His Son: Jesus Christ. It is a *free gift* God bestows on *"everyone who calls on the name of the Lord"* (cf. Romans 10:9-13, Joel 2:32). He then gives them a new nature; but for our entire natural lives, we must yet contend with the old nature (Romans 7:14-25).

Once we have a new nature as believers, how are we to live? How do we understand God and ourselves in relation to God and to those around us? We understand the nature of God, and what He expects of us through reading the unchanging Word of God. In his last letter to the young pastor Timothy, the Apostle Paul describes the whole of Scripture as sufficient for the task.

> *All Scripture is breathed out by God and profitable for teaching, for reproof, for correction, and for training in righteousness, that the man of God may be complete, equipped for every good work.* (2 Timothy 3:16-17)

According to the Apostle, *everything* we need to be complete and fully equipped in faith and practice is found in the God-breathed, inspired Scripture. How is it appropriated? He tells the young pastor Timothy a few verses earlier:

You, however, have followed my teaching, my conduct, my

aim in life, my faith, my patience, my love, my steadfastness,
(2 Timothy 3:10)

The Apostle cites three elements of what we might think of as discipleship in the faith: Sound scriptural teaching, observation, and imitation. We see these three factors at work in the New Testament regarding the life of Timothy. Timothy learned the Word of God from his faithful teacher and mentor—the Apostle Paul. Timothy observed the Apostle Paul's Christ-centered doctrine and resulting conduct, and he understood Paul's aim or purpose in life. He witnessed Paul's grace, patience, exhibition of love, steadfastness, and perseverance in spite of persecutions and even life-threatening events. Timothy was to remember Paul's teachings, to imitate those behaviors he learned from Paul, and pass them on to others (2 Timothy 2:2).

Paul's admonitions to this young pastor apply with equal force to pastors and leaders today. Still we find the newest rage sweeping the evangelical church at the moment is the Enneagram. Celebrity pastors are endorsing it. Megachurches are taking their staff through Enneagram training and then teaching it to their congregations during the Sunday morning services and/or small groups. Yet, it is being touted as *the* invaluable "spiritual tool." How then, did the Apostles Peter and Paul or Jesus, for that matter, not know anything about it?

The Enneagram: What is it?

The word *enneagram* comes from two Greek words: ἐννέα (ennéa), which translates as *nine* and γράμμα (grámma), which translates to something *written* or *drawn*. It is drawn as a circle with nine points which are connected with lines (see following figure).

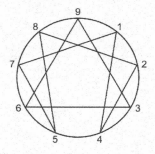

Current Version of the Enneagram

It is dubbed as "sacred" by author Chris L. Heuertz, and supposedly provides each person with their own unique spiritual path.[9] Authors Ion Cron and Suzanne Stabile tell their readers where the path of the Enneagram leads: It is *"The Road Back to You."*[10] Richard Rohr, Franciscan priest and primary promoter and discipler of the Enneagram, writes:

> The whole Enneagram diagram is called "the face of God." If you could look out at reality from nine pairs of eyes and honor all of them, you would look at reality through the eyes of God.[11]

In an interview in *Religious News Service*, Chris Heuertz explains it isn't promoted as a personality typing system which explains why you (and others) do what you do. He expounds:

> One of my teachers, Russ Hudson[12] says, "Type isn't a 'type' of person, but a path to God." I believe it's sacred because as a map of our soul it's a compassionate sketch of possibilities. The Enneagram is less about nine "types of people" and more about nine paths back to our true selves and nine paths to divine love.[13]

It is claimed the reason you act as you do and those around you act as they do is because all people are currently living as their "false self." The goal is to get you on the "sacred" spiritual path—on *"The Road Back to You."* Each of the numbers is used somewhat differently depending on who the particular "spiritual director" happens to be. Generally, they are classified as follows:

1	Reformer	The Perfectionist	The Need to be Perfect
2	Helper	The Giver	The Need to be Needed
3	Achiever	The Performer	The Need to Succeed
4	Individualist	The Romantic	The Need to be Special / Unique
5	Investigator	The Observer	The Need to Perceive / Understand
6	Loyalist	The Loyal Skeptic	The Need to be Sure / Certain
7	Enthusiast	The Epicure	The Need to Avoid Pain
8	Challenger	The Protector	The Need to be Against
9	Peacemaker	The Mediator	The Need to Avoid

For those who think the Enneagram sounds like a personal or corporate self-improvement tool, it is not. Richard Rohr is direct on answering that question:

> The purpose of the Enneagram is not self-improvement, which would be our ego's goal. Rather, it is the transformation of consciousness so that we can realize our essence, our True Self.[14]

Why does teaching the Enneagram seem to be growing in the evangelical church? Again, Chris Heuertz gives an opinion:

> I sort of wonder if the evolved evangelical is getting a little worn out from the same old literal Bible study interpretations of stuff. At least Catholicism can appeal to tradition and saints. I wonder if some evangelicals have gotten bored with what their tradition offers, and therefore, they find a deeper and more contemplative system like the Enneagram appealing.[15]

Several of the promoters and proponents of the Enneagram instruct individuals to look within themselves for true spiritual understanding and growth. In order to appeal to Christians, to whom all this verbiage might sound foreign and raise their suspicion, they attempt to provide a credible-sounding, historical Christian basis for the Enneagram by alluding to or cherry-picking partial quotes from reformer John Calvin's book *Institutes of the Christian Religion*. For example, in *The Road Back to You: An Enneagram Journey to Self-Discovery*, co-author Ian Cron relates a conversation he had with "Brother Dave." A friend had encouraged Cron to meet him and described "Brother Dave" as a "75 year-old Benedictine monk and spiritual director."[16] While extolling the benefits of the Enneagram, "Brother Dave" tells him of "the importance of self-knowledge on the spiritual path."[17] Cron writes:

> How, as John Calvin put it, "without knowledge of self, there is no knowledge of God."[18]

You don't have to be a Calvinist to know John Calvin did not promote the use of the Enneagram, and he'd be astonished he was taken out of context in this way. Calvin's "knowledge of self" idea was the knowledge that:

> the infinitude of good which resides in God becomes more apparent from our poverty. In particular, the miserable ruin into which the revolt of the first man has plunged us, ... in short, depravity and corruption[19]

In short, Calvin asserted that *we are sinners in need of a savior!* A simple reading of the Bible gives us sufficient knowledge of our "true self" to understand that in our current state (still on this Earth, not yet glorified), our heart with the old, sinful nature is *"deceitful above all things and desperately wicked: who can know it?"* (Jeremiah 17:9). According to the teachers of the Enneagram, they prefer and promote a knowledge of ourselves that comes from within ourselves and not from Scripture. From there, Franciscan priest Richard Rohr, who has contributed much towards the wild popularity of the Enneagram, extrapolates that into meaning that in order to have true self-knowledge, we need to get in touch with "our true self."

Let's look a little closer into where John Calvin and his disciples were actually going with the "self-knowledge" he advocated in book 1, chapter 1 of his *Institutes*. Calvin's view can be summed up in three points.

The first point is: Without knowledge of self, there is no knowledge of God. As Calvin pondered this point, he was trying to sort out which comes first—a true knowledge of self or a true knowledge of God? Do we recognize our utterly bankrupt, evil nature and the good gifts which come from God by self-examination? Or does seeing the holiness and goodness of God expose us to a true knowledge of ourselves by contrast? He writes:

> For as there exists in man something like a world of misery, and ever since we were stript [sic] of the divine attire our naked shame discloses an immense series of disgraceful properties every man, being stung by the consciousness of his own unhappiness, in this way necessarily obtains at least some knowledge of God. Thus, our feeling of ignorance,

vanity, want, weakness, in short, depravity and corruption, reminds us [see Calvin on John 4:10], that in the Lord, and none but He, dwell the true light of wisdom, solid virtue, exuberant goodness.[20]

In point two, he writes:

> it is evident that man never attains to a true self-knowledge until he has previously contemplated the face of God and come down after such contemplation to look into himself. For (such is our innate pride) we always seem to ourselves just, and upright, and wise, and holy, until we are convinced, by clear evidence, of our injustice, vileness, folly, and impurity. ... He being the only standard by the application of which this conviction can be produced.[21]

When we compare ourselves with ourselves, we may look pretty good *to* ourselves. But that is a pretty low standard. It is only when we compare ourselves to the utterly righteous and just God, that we realize we are lost and undone, knowing we have nothing whatsoever to offer Him. According to Calvin, what provides the "clear evidence" to convince us of our true self? In point 3, he writes:

> Hence that dread and amazement with which as Scripture uniformly relates, holy men were struck and overwhelmed whenever they beheld the presence of God. When we see those who previously stood firm and secure so quaking with terror, that the fear of death takes hold of them, nay, they are, in a manner, swallowed up and annihilated, the inference to be drawn is that men are never duly touched and impressed with a conviction of their insignificance, until they have contrasted themselves with the majesty of God.[22]

Those who are heavily involved in promoting and teaching the Enneagram may truly desire to help people. But, do they teach truth regarding the question of the nature of human beings? Are human beings, as they suggest, basically good and innocent, but damaged in early childhood; and do people basically need to get back to their undamaged "true self"? Or is every one of us, as Scripture clearly teaches and Calvin reiterates, unholy sinners by nature who quake "with terror" when "they have contrasted themselves with the majesty of God?" According to what God tells us in Scripture:

> *The fear of the LORD is the beginning of wisdom, and the knowledge of the Holy One is insight.* (Proverbs 9:10)

If the spiritual directors of the Enneagram are wrong on this *essential, foundational point* regarding the *true nature of mankind*, how does that impact their views and their trustworthiness on the essentials of the historic Christian faith overall? Do the Enneagram teachings pass the scriptural litmus test in the area of the essentials of the Christian faith? Are the teachers, authors, promoters, and pastors directing us to the God-breathed Word of God to which the Apostle Paul points *"for teaching, for reproof, for correction, and for training in righteousness"* (2 Timothy 3:16)?

CHAPTER 3

Myth Taken

As I urged you when I was going to Macedonia, remain at Ephesus so that you may charge certain persons not to teach any different doctrine, nor to devote themselves to myths and endless genealogies, which promote speculations rather than the stewardship from God that is by faith. (1 Timothy 1:3-4, The Apostle Paul)

The Apostle Paul was *very* concerned about correct doctrine. *Doctrine* is an unpopular word to some Christians today, who have come to think of doctrine as divisive and not as relevant to their lives. Doctrine *is* divisive in one sense: It divides truth from error! Truly, there is nothing *more relevant* to a Christian's life than staying *in the faith!* The teaching of sound doctrine keeps people spiritually protected from wandering away from the faith and into serious error.

In Acts 20:28-30, the Apostle Paul charged the Ephesian elders to *"Pay careful attention to yourselves"* and to watch over the flock. They were to guard themselves and the flock against spiritual predators who would attempt to invade the church from the outside and from within. In Acts 20:30, he told them, *"from among your*

45

own selves will arise men speaking twisted things, to draw away the
disciples after them."

Three years later, he penned a letter to the young Pastor Timothy of the church in Ephesus, Paul's *"true child in the faith"* (1
Timothy 1:2). Paul began by reminding Timothy of why he had
"urged" Timothy to remain behind in Paul's stead. Timothy was
to *"charge"* (i.e., command or declare to) *"certain persons"* (who
are not named in the text) to stop teaching *"different"* (i.e., strange,
novel, or unusual) doctrine. It appears these false teachers were not
outsiders but were operating within the church:

> It is true that "there is no indication that those who were
> spreading false doctrine were outsiders," but neither is there
> indication that they were accepted congregational leaders.
> They may have been quite on the fringe but with influence
> over some in the congregation through personal relationships
> or other means, of which commentators at this remove have
> no knowledge.[1]

The false teachers were veering away from sound, essential
doctrines of the faith and were leading others astray. They were
gaining a following by portraying themselves as revealing ancient
mystical wisdom and other early heresies. *Vine's Complete Exposi-*
tory Dictionary of Old and New Testament Words comments on the
word *myths*:

> The word is used of gnostic errors and of Jewish and pro-
> fane fables and genealogies, in 1 Timothy 1:4; 4:7; 2 Timothy
> 4:4; Titus 1:14; of fiction, in 2 Peter 1:16.[2]

The ancient Hebrew culture properly used genealogies to re-
count the history of human origins and development. With the land
promises made to Abraham and later to Moses, genealogies were
important to Jacob and his descendants in order to keep track of
which tribe owned what land.[3] They were also used, as we see in the
Gospel accounts, to demonstrate the royal blood line of succession:

> Genealogical records were used, furthermore, to establish
> and maintain the right of royal succession in the southern king-

dom. Here descent from the house of David was the important
consideration, and when the prophets began to teach that the
Messiah would emerge from that stock (cf. Isa. 11:1–5), such
genealogies immediately became far more significant than before. As a result, it is hardly surprising that in the NT great
care was taken to establish Jesus' lineal descent from David.[4]

Why was Timothy being reminded and instructed to confront
this group publicly? They positioned themselves as having special
spiritual knowledge to impart to others. They gained a following by
spinning tales concerning the origins of that knowledge and, perhaps, by explaining why they happen to have this superior authori-
tative knowledge when others do not. The problems were that the
stories were *false*, the origins questionable or non-existent, and the
doctrines heretical.

Enneagram's Alleged Certificate of Authenticity

The current spates of books circulating in the evangelical
church offers up pretty much the same story to establish a genealogical pedigree. The narrative is used to persuade others that the
Enneagram is rooted in Christian history. Christopher L. Heuertz,
in his book *The Sacred Enneagram: Finding Your Unique Path to
Spiritual Growth* (foreword by Franciscan Priest Richard Rohr),
proposes the possibility the Enneagram was in use in other ancient
non-Jewish and non-Christian cultures and mystical religions. Some
of the "evidence" cited is from New Age sources such as Beatrice
Chestnut (1964-), a student of New Agers Helen Palmer and Dr.
David Daniels (1934-2017):

Chestnut's claims might be found in Homer's epic poem,
The Odyssey:

> Perhaps the oldest recorded hint of the Enneagram may
> be in what Beatrice Chestnut speculates to be evidence hidden
> away in Homer's classic work, *The Odyssey*.
> One of the first written texts in [W]estern literature, *The
> Odyssey* tells the story of the metaphoric journey "home" to
> the "[T]rue [S]elf." In the story, the hero, Odysseus (the guy
> who thought up the "Trojan Horse"), returning home from

the Trojan War, travels to nine "lands" populated with mythic creatures whose characters match the nine Enneagram types exactly—in the same order as the modern teaching![5]

While it might be interesting, the real problem with this claim is: It is not true. It appears to have been *crafted* to fit the Enneagram story. There is nothing in the epic tale about searching, finding, or returning to the hero's "True Self." The story line is about a ten-year struggle to return home after the Trojan War. As it turns out, Odysseus didn't travel to nine lands but rather 12 (13 if you count his homeland and 14 if you count his starting point). After departing Troy, the lands he traveled to are:

1.   The Island of the Cicones
2.   The Island of the Lotus Eaters
3.   The Island of the Cyclops
4.   The Island of Aeolus
5.   The Island of the Laestrygonians
6.   Circe's Island
7.   The Underworld
8.   The Island of the Sirens
9.   Scylla and Charybdis
10. The Island of Helios
11. Ogygia (Calypso's Island)
12. The Island of the Phaecians
13. (Arrive Ithaca)

Finally, Odysseus arrives at his home in Ithaca. It would seem Christopher Heuertz may simply have taken Beatrice Chestnut's word for the veracity of the "nine lands" claim, but this falsehood is being fobbed off on the unwary as fact in an attempt to establish some historical credibility for the Enneagram.

Christopher Heuertz continues his endeavor to build a genealogical history by suggesting the Greek philosopher Pythagoras (c. B.C. 570-495):

is said to have used a drawing resembling the Enneagram symbol as his spiritual signature after learning of it in Heliopolis, which was the center of worship of the Ennead or the nine deities of ancient Egyptian mythology.[6]

It is unclear as to who supposedly "said" this; but again, this is a mythical claim since:

No authentic writings of Pythagoras have survived.[7]

If no authentic writings of Pythagoras have survived, then the mythical "spiritual signature" cannot be authoritatively "said" to have been used.

What About the People of God?

Heuertz's Enneagram genealogy moves on from non-Jewish and pre-Christian sources to claim its use among the people of God before the advent of the Messiah. He writes:

> Others point to the Jewish philosopher Philo (who also happened to live in Egypt), hinting that perhaps his esoteric Judaism and the Tree of Life, which is considered the key symbol of the tradition of the Kabbalah, root the earliest forms of the Enneagram in Jewish mysticism.[8]

Notice his use of assumptive language: "hinting that perhaps." In other words, we have *no actual evidence*. Again, some undefined and undocumented "others" are attributed with *making the suggestion* that Philo "perhaps" *may* have made use of it. Whether this is true or not, at this point, becomes secondary. Use of the occult Kabbalah should automatically exclude it from consideration by any Bible believing and teaching church. Why? It is an appeal to mystical occultism:

> Kabbalah is a body of mystical and esoteric beliefs based on commentaries on the Torah, the first five books of Hebrew Scripture (Genesis to Deuteronomy). The term *kabbalah* comes from a Hebrew root word, *kbl*, which means "to receive." The Jewish Talmud, a collection of ancient Rabbinic writings, teaches that the secrets of Kabbalah are to be "carefully controlled."[9]

Why would the esoteric practices of Kabbalah—reading hidden

meaning into the biblical text—be offered as evidence of legitimacy that the Enneagram should be used by the people of God? Rather than recommend its use, the Bible very clearly identifies use of practices like the Enneagram and other such teachings as something to be shunned by believers in the God of the Bible (cf. Jeremiah 14:14).

Now we come to the post-Nicene Christian church era (after the Council of Nicaea in 325 A.D.). Was the Enneagram a spiritual tool in use in Christian circles by that time at least? According to Christopher Heuertz:

> Much has been written to suggest that the early Egyptian Christian monastic ascetics, the desert mothers and fathers, were the chief architects of the Enneagram, led by the fourth-century mystic Evagrius Ponticus. Ponticus's writings are often cited to support theories on the Christian origins of the Enneagram, specifically as it relates to his work on his list of eight vices and virtues (in one place he names nine), which closely resemble the nine Virtues and Passions of the Enneagram as we have it today.[10]

Now, if you should wonder exactly where "Much has been written to suggest" this theory, you won't have to look far. It cannot be found *anywhere* in what little we have of the writings of Ponticus or copies of his works. Yes, Evagrius Ponticus was a mystic who believed we:

> can find reconciliation only by an ascetical, self-mortifying process whereby the spirit regains its rule over matter and realizes its capacity to experience the divine simplicity.[11]

For Heuertz, the source for the claim that Evagrius Ponticus was one of the "chief architects of the Enneagram" is Franciscan Priest Richard Rohr along with Andreas Ebert (1952-), his co-author of the book *The Enneagram: A Christian Perspective* (2001). Richard Rohr is the individual who has trained, discipled, and continues to teach the current popular authors who are writing about the Enneagram for evangelical publishers. Other than this citation parroting Rohr's unsubstantiated claims, no actual evidence is given. But what of the claim? Was there a cadre of mystic Christian "monastic ascetics, the desert mothers and fathers" following, "the fourth-century mystic Evagrius Ponticus" providing us with at least a *possible* certificate of authenticity for the Enneagram dating to their time?

The Evagrius Connection

The claim that the Enneagram goes back to Evagrius of Pontus (345-399 A.D.) and the Desert Fathers and Mothers is fantasy at best and contrived at worst. It is not necessarily Christopher L. Heuertz's fantasy, but it is fantasy nonetheless. The claim is based on Richard Rohr and Andreas Ebert's misinterpretation of a single passage in the writings of Evagrius from which the two authors imagined Evagrius was trying to describe an actual diagram. The biblically astute are familiar with the phrase "Context is King" when it comes to reading and understanding Scripture. However, the same is true with *anything* we read. The historical-grammatical context—how words and language were used during a particular historical time and setting—helps us understand what different writers were actually communicating when they wrote. Evagrius was simply speaking in a way that was very common among Christians of his day in describing what was thought of as the "shape" of numbers. Rohr and Ebert imagined that Evagrius had an actual geometrical diagram in mind in his writing which contained the number "shapes" he was describing; but they simply were confused. To be sure, it would be possible to fudge together a kind of enneagram (nine-point diagram) from some of the number-shapes Evagrius mentions. The closest example one could come up with would look something like this:

An Imaginary Figure

But in its historical-grammatical context, that isn't what Evagri-us was doing. He was just following the usual way of interpreting numbers common to Christian writers at the time. It would appear Rohr and Ebert were not sufficiently familiar with the practices of Patristic writers to understand what was going on in the Evagrius passage. However, is it possible and, perhaps, probable that Rohr and Ebert were in search of genealogical validation of their claims, and their conclusion is a result of what Ronald V. Huggins, Th.D., describes as:

> promiscuously fishing about in the Patristic texts for some support, any support, they might find for their Enneagram symbol along with its attendant personality test. The predictable result was that they anachronistically read both their symbol and the test back into this single passage in Evagrius. And the whole Enneagram community uncritically took over their idea. In reality the Enneagram symbol cannot be shown to predate 1916, and the link between the symbol and the text can be fairly confidently dated as occurring for the first time in c. 1969.[12]

Even though Rohr and Ebert currently suggest the idea that the Enneagram had Christian roots at least back to Evagrius, which they arrived at through the aforementioned misinterpretation of a single short passage by Evagrius, the mythology becomes murkier. In fact, it is of interest that Rohr and Ebert did not claim a Christian origin for the Enneagram in the earlier edition of their book. Ebert writes in the 1992 introduction to Richard Rohr and Andreas Ebert's *Discovering the Enneagram: An Ancient Tool for a New Spiritual Journey* (trans. Peter Heinegg; New York: Crossroad, 1992):

> The Enneagram is a mysterious model of the psyche that is <u>not originally Christian</u>. (pg.xiii)

> I believe that the Enneagram can help us to find a deeper and more authentic relationship with God—even though it was <u>not discovered by Christians</u>. (pg.xv)[13]

Again, it is important to note that in 1992, according to Rohr and Ebert, the Enneagram was "not originally Christian" and "not discovered by Christians."

Sketchy Origins

Even though Richard Rohr and Andreas Ebert's 1992 book admitted there is *no Christian connection* "originally" and that it was "not discovered by Christians," Rohr and, subsequently, his disciples point not only to Evagrius, but also to a thirteenth-century "mathematician, polymath, philosopher, logician, Franciscan tertiary and writer ..,"[14] Ramon Llull (1232/33-1315/16). One very accessible instance is Rohr's endorsement on the website of New Ager, Helen Palmer:

> Helen Palmer teaches the Enneagram with an in-depth and clinical clarity that can only help and strengthen those who are seeking to use it for spiritual direction, Christian guidance, or even the classic "reading of souls". [sic] She is standing on the 13th Century [sic] teaching of my fellow Franciscan, Blessed Raymond Lull, [sic, Ramón Llull] who successfully used the ancient Enneagram as a lingua franca to mutually evangelize warring Christians and Moslems. This is a very proven, traditional, and tested tool for both the "conversion of morals", [sic] and the "discernment of spirits" which St. Paul calls one of the major Gifts of the Holy Spirit (1 Corinthians 12:10).[15]

Rohr's words may seem reassuring to those interested in the Enneagram. After all, if Ramón Llull "successfully used" the Enneagram to "evangelize warring Christians and Moslems," who could possibly object to such a powerful spiritual tool? We are assured by Rohr that Christians can take comfort that a New Ager, Helen Palmer, can provide them with "Christian guidance." After all, she is standing on the teaching of Rohr's "fellow Franciscan, Blessed Raymond Lull." And if, as Rohr claims Llull allegedly suggests, even the Apostle Paul would be in favor of this "very proven, traditional, and tested tool," how could we have a better recommendation?

As simply and kindly as we are able, we must point out the

assertion is false. As Richard Rohr and Andreas Ebert stated in the introduction of their 1992 book on the subject, the Enneagram was "not originally Christian" and "was not discovered by Christians." So, how did the newly minted Enneagram "Directors" make the connection between Llull and the Enneagram? In order to explain, we should take a moment to point out something which should be obvious about geometric shapes. All you need to do to make an enneagram (as opposed to *the* Enneagram as we know it) is to overlay three triangles in the same sort of way that you do to get a hexagram (Star of David) by overlapping two triangles.

It is true that Llull drew *many* diagrams overlaying all sorts of different geometric shapes including a number of them that primarily involved triangles. So, for example, he created symbols around one, two, three, five, nine, fourteen and sixteen triangles which contained 3, 6, 9, 14, 15, and 16 points. But none of these, nor any of his other symbols, represent the symbol we recognize today as the Enneagram. While it is true that what Llull drew made use of geometric designs as does the Enneagram, that does not connect his diagrams to the Enneagram. Llull knew *nothing* of the Enneagram, and there is *zero evidence* he used the symbol in evangelizing Muslims or Christians.

The myth Christopher L. Heuertz recites in order to present the Enneagram as a Christian spiritual tool is built on the claims of New Agers, Kabbalists, mystics, and then finally, Sufis are included:

> Very commonly, many of today's experts credit Sufi communities spread throughout Central Asia, from Iraq to Afghanistan, for developing the Enneagram between the thirteenth and sixteenth centuries.[16]

Sufis are an Islamic mystical religion. Again, we have to ask, why would any Christian go to the mystical arm of Islam for Christian guidance? Is "Sola Scriptura" (Scripture alone) insufficient for faith and practice? What Heuertz says next should stop every reader in their tracks:

> Regardless of whether the Enneagram has its roots in Buddhism, Judaism, Christianity, or Islam, we do know that it wasn't until the early 1900s that an Eastern Orthodox man,

G.I. Gurdjieff, introduced the modern form of the Enneagram to the Western world.[17]

After spending a considerable amount of time laying out a supposed ancient history, Heuretz essentially admits it is all a myth. He doesn't actually know if it "has its roots in Buddhism, Judaism, Christianity, or Islam." So why the story? It's about supposed credibility. Heuertz points out "we do know" the only *certain history* of the Enneagram begins with a man named G.I. Gurdjieff, who we will meet in our next chapter.

Self-proclaimed "Champion of the Enneagram"[18] Ian Cron (1960-) is more direct and straightforward after reciting a similar history in his book with Suzanne Stabile (1961-) *The Road Back to You: An Enneagram Journey to Self-Discovery*:

> If its <u>sketchy origins</u> weren't enough to <u>spook the mules,</u> <u>there is no scientific evidence that proves the Enneagram is a</u> <u>reliable measurement of personality</u>. Who cares that millions of people thought it was accurate? Grizzly man thought he could make friends with bears and we know how that turned out.[19]

The Enneagram has "sketchy origins," which could "spook the mules." If the church was heeding the Apostle Paul's fervent warnings about false teachers and false doctrines, the sketchy origins—from pagan, New Age sources, and Islam—would certainly "spook the mules" exactly as it *absolutely should*. Others have tried to track down evidence for each of the above claims, and none was found. A dedicated adherent to the non-Christian version of the Enneagram, Jim Aldrich (aka "RunningSon"), admits this is the case:

> Consider James Webb: no independent scholar worked more doggedly to unearth the provenance of Gurdjieff's ideas. Yet all his efforts to tease the enneagram out of cognate materia in the Kabbalah, in the *Ars Magna* of Ramón Lull (c. 1232-1315), and the *Arithmologia* of the Jesuit Athanasius Kircher (1601-1680), seem finally as implausible as they are laboured. Consider J. G. Bennett: no Gurdjieffian became more personally and passionately involved in the search. Yet his convolut-

ed argument that the enneagram 'originated with the Sarmãn society about 2500 years ago and was revised when the power of the Arabic numeral system was developed in Samarkand in the fifteenth century', [sic] is projected with no hint of intellectual vigilance, and supported by no scrap of textual or archaeological evidence.

Conclusion: although some future revelation cannot be ruled out, we may meanwhile decently hypothesise [sic] that the enneagram is sui generis and G.I. Gurdjieff, if not its author, is at least its first modern proponent.[20]

Remember, Cron also admitted in his previous quote "there is no scientific evidence that proves the Enneagram is a reliable measurement of personality."

What we have so far with the Enneagram are "myths" taken as truth of the kind the Apostle Paul instructed the young Pastor Timothy to put a stop to publicly. To another young pastor named Titus, Paul wrote:

For there are many who are insubordinate, empty talkers and deceivers, especially those of the circumcision party. **They must be silenced,** *since they are upsetting whole families by teaching for shameful gain what they ought not to teach.* (Titus 1:10-11) [emphasis added]

CHAPTER 4

Genesis of the Enneagram:
From Gurdjieff to Rohr

In the beginning was the Word, and the Word was with God, and the Word was God. He was in the beginning with God. All things were made through him, and without him was not anything made that was made. (John 1:1-3)

The Apostle John penned the opening lines of his Gospel in response to the false claims of an early heresy called Docetism:

An early Christian heresy associated with *Gnosticism, docetism [sic] denied the material nature of Christ and thus his true humanity. The term is derived from the Greek word *dokeo*, which means "to seem," or "to appear," and thus a docetic view would be that Christ only appeared to be human.[1]

In John 1, John addresses several key areas of essential doctrines of the faith including origins, the nature of God, the nature of man, and the nature of redemption. He does so in several ways. He lays out what God has already revealed down through history, and which has been the biblical teaching on these issues. He begins with origins by pointing back to Genesis 1: *"In the beginning,"* whenever the beginning was, the Word already was; and to make certain the reader understands, he defines what that means: The Word existed with God, was *"with"* God face-to-face (*with* here is English for the Greek word *pros* which means *one as always turned toward one*); and, in fact, the Word is God Himself. Creation was brought into existence by the Word. Creation was not a series of accidents and errors by lesser beings, it wasn't the result of a different, inferior creator; these beliefs are the seeds of what would later become Gnosticism. *The International Standard Bible Encyclopedia, Revised* comments:

> *Gospel of John* Some regard Jn. 19:34f as a personal protest against Gnosticism. After describing the piercing of Christ's side by the soldier's spear, and how "at once there came out blood and water," the apostle adds, "He who saw it has borne witness—his testimony is true, and he knows that he tells the truth—that you also may believe." Other passages seem to be directed against Docetism, e.g., "And the Word became flesh and dwelt among us ... we have beheld his glory" (1:14). This is, perhaps, the most convincing statement of all (cf. also 4:6 and 20:27).[2]

John states emphatically in John 1:3, *if* He (the Word) did not create something, it does not exist. If it *was* created, He is the one Who created it. In 29 short verses, the Apostle lays out Who God is, how Creation was *accomplished*, and that God incarnated in human form and secured redemption. *He* created everything. *He* incarnated in human flesh (John 1:14). *He* is the Christ Who provided redemption (John 1:29). *He* is the *"true light"* (John 1:9-10).

> *But to all who did receive him, who believed in his name, he gave the right to become children of God, who were born, not of blood nor of the will of the flesh nor of the will of man, but of God. And the Word became flesh and dwelt among us, and we have seen his glory, glory as of the only Son from the Father, full of grace and truth.* (John 1:12-14)

In the second century, one Early Church Father Irenaeus, spent a great deal of time refuting many of these same errors in his *Against Heresies,* where he writes:

For when John, proclaiming one God, the Almighty, and one Jesus Christ, the Only-begotten [*monogenes* in Greek], by whom all things were made, declares that this was the Son of God, this the Only-begotten, this the Former of all things, this the true Light who enlighteneth every man, this the Creator of the world, this He that came to His own, this He that became flesh and dwelt among us,—these men, by a plausible kind of exposition, perverting these statements, maintain that there was another Monogenes [only-begotten], according to production, whom they also style Arche [*beginning, origin* in English]. They also maintain that there was another Saviour, and another Logos [*Word* in English], the son of Monogenes, and another Christ[3] [brackets, clarification added]

Heresies do not give up easily. They morph, twist, adapt, and resurface from time to time throughout history; and they must be recognized and dealt with biblically.

A New Cosmic Story

The book of Genesis, to which John pointed back, *is* God's revelation to us which unequivocally asserts He created the universe; therefore, we have a sure word on that.

Everything created has a beginning. What is the genesis of the Enneagram? The Enneagram is created. It did not exist prior to Creation, and it did not spring from nothing. As we have previously pointed out (see chapter 3), there is no record of its use among God's people or, indeed, any other culture or religion in ancient times. Jesus, Paul, and the other Apostles were not aware of it; so, from where did the Enneagram originate?

Christopher Heuertz gives a nod to the lack of evidence in history and points to the person whom he says "we do know" introduced it: George Ivanovich Gurdjieff:

Regardless of whether the Enneagram has its roots in Buddhism, Judaism, Christianity, or Islam, we do know that it wasn't until the early 1900s that an Eastern Orthodox man, G. I. Gurdjieff, introduced the modern form of the Enneagram to the Western world.[4]

It began with merely a nine-sided diagram inscribed inside a circle, which was devised by George I. Gurdjieff (1866?-1949), an esoteric teacher.

The Original Enneagram by George I. Gurdjieff

According to early disciple and Russian esotericist P. D. Ouspensky,[5] Gurdjieff taught the Enneagram was a knowledge of all that is in the cosmos.

> All knowledge can be included in the enneagram and with the help of the enneagram it can be interpreted. And in this connection only what a man is able to put into the enneagram does he actually *know*, that is, understand. What he cannot put into the enneagram makes books and libraries entirely unnecessary. *Everything* can be included and read in the enneagram.[6]

Gurdjieff believed all the secret laws of the universe could be seen in his diagram, and he used it to play around with mathematical formulas—what he called the "Law of Seven" and the "Law of Three." He also used the Enneagram to illustrate a special musical scale for which he developed "sacred dance" movements to act out the Enneagram, which Gurdjieff dance troupes still use today.[7] However, it was *never* used for character or personality assessment by its inventor, George I. Gurdjieff.

Gurdjieff and his followers claimed he had traveled and gleaned wisdom from other faiths, but none of the claims are verified. Some of his followers asserted Gurdjieff had contact with a secret Sufi brotherhood; but again, there is no historical evidence for the existence of such a group.[8] Even so, his "sacred dance movement" employed a whirling-dervish-type dancer[9] right in front of an Enneagram.

Gurdjieff, like many esoteric spiritual teachers of his day, blended ideas from different sources, came up with his own theories, and gathered followers who came to believe in his ideas. Although raised as Eastern Orthodox, Gurdjieff had rejected those teachings in favor of formulating his own spiritual views which were called "esoteric Christianity."[10] Gurdjieff believed man is not aware of true reality and needs an awakening of consciousness. According to *Larson's Book of World Religions and Alternative Spirituality*:

> Gurdjieff sought to open up man's consciousness to higher planes of awareness. He believed that most people are "asleep," but they can be "awakened" by having a greater sense of self-awareness. Then they will be able to see the various egos and proceed to seek out which part of them is the real "I."
>
> This "Fourth Way," as it is called, is the path of self-transformation. Seekers are encouraged to begin each morning concentrating on putting the "self" into each part of their bodies, beginning with the toes and so on. Eventually "self-consciousness" enables one constantly to observe his body and become aware of unconscious mannerisms.
>
> The purpose of such exercises is to shatter the illusion that reactions and intentions are a choice of free will. The next goal is obtaining "objective consciousness," by which a person finally discovers his true self. Human effort thus enables us to "save" his own soul.[11]

A true understanding of ourselves, or what we might refer to as "self-awareness," comes from understanding and applying scriptural truths accompanied by sound biblical teaching. God works in us revealing weaknesses that often manifest in sinful behavior which God empowers us to change. For instance, a young woman becomes engaged to a young man who is godly, but he is unaware of some hurtful patterns in his responses to her. These will not be revealed by a questionnaire or some special spiritual experience such as through the Enneagram. Rather, godly counsel or even rebuke in conjunction with the application of the truth of God's Word is needed.

However, it is typical of mystical and New Age beliefs that humanity needs to awaken to new perceptions, a new conscious-ness, and realize a "true self." Gurdjieff had great influence on the modern New Age movement. Marcia Montenegro, co-author of this book, was well-aware of him when she was an adherent of the New Age Movement and its practices.

It was left to Gurdjieff's pupil, P. D. Ouspensky to write about Gurdjieff's teachings, including the Enneagram (Ouspensky's books were published postmortem). One portion of the Enneagram as used today, the Triads (three areas of the Enneagram), seems to be based on Gurdjieff's Law of Three as found in Ouspensky's book *In Search of the Miraculous.* According to *Theology Thinktank*'s article by Brandon Medina:

> Gurdjieff believed that throughout history there were three traditional modes of transferring our identity from the temporal (bound by time and space) to the immortal:
> - The way of the fakir (the way of struggle with the physical body).
> - The way of the monk (the way of faith, the emotional way).
> - The way of the yogi (the way of knowledge, the way of mind).[12]

Up to this point, these various teachings had nothing to do with personality or temperament. It appears the first person to attempt to employ the Enneagram in this manner was "esoteric Christian" Rodney Collin (1909-1956), who authored *The Christian Mystery* in 1954[13] and was a follower of Gurdjieff and Ouspensky.

> Collin, inspired by medieval alchemy and medicine and also the work of Dr. Berman, linked each gland in the human endocrine system with the influence of a particular planet. By assigning dominant centers of gravity of different people in distinct glandular manifestations, he arrived at six central planetary types and variable subdivisions thereof.[14]

He created the diagram of "The Types of Humanity:"

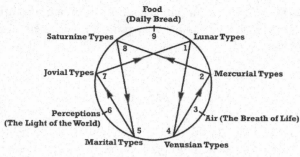

Fig. 12: The Types of Humanity

First (1954) "Types of Humanity" suggested by Rodney Collin

Dr. Ronald V. Huggins (1951-) B.F.A., Th.D., formerly of Moody Bible Institute (Spokane), Salt Lake Theological Seminary, and Midwestern Baptist Theological Seminary, adds:

> In 1954, Rodney Collin, a student of P.D. Ouspensky, became perhaps the first to make a stab at linking personality types to an enneagram. Starting with the ancient idea that personalities originate due to planetary influences, the mercurial personality from Mercury, the jovial personality from Jove (Jupiter), the martial personality with Mars, and so on, Collin adopted the traditional view that personality is fixed by the position of the planets at birth. But he went on to claim that when we arrange these planetary personality types around an enneagram, it allows us to view humanity as a single whole through which a kind of movement flows like the circulation of blood through the body. Collin claimed that once you've become firmly cognizant of your own planetary personality type, you can improve yourself by trying to incorporate elements from the first two planetary types, as it were, downstream in the enneagram flow sequence from your own according to the formula 142857. So, for example, if you are a martial type (point 5 on Collin's enneagram), you can improve yourself by incorporating features first from the Jovial type (point 7), and then second from the Lunar type, representing "cool instinctive certainty" (point 1). Similarly, if you are a Jovial

type (point 7), you can improve yourself by incorporating fea-
tures first from the Lunar type (point 1), and then second the
Venusian (Venus) type (point 4), and so on around with all the
types.[15]

From Esoteric Gnosticism to New Age Occultism

The Enneagram arrived at the doorstep of an occult teacher, Bo-
livian Oscar Ichazo, who taught it at the Arica Institute—the school
he founded in 1968 in Arica, Chile. There are conflicting stories
about how Ichazo learned the Enneagram; as a result, we have no
verified explanation of this. His claim of recognition of it as a tool
in 1954 seems to coincide with Rodney Collin's work. Even his
initial views seem to parallel those of Collin:

> Ichazo indicated the three basic human instincts for sur-
> vival: "conservation" (the digestive system); "relation" (the
> circulatory system) and "adaptation" (the central nervous sys-
> tem); and two poles of attraction to self-perpetuation: "sexual"
> (the sexual organs) and "spiritual" (the spinal column).[16]

A student there, psychiatrist and New Age spiritual seeker
Claudio Naranjo, as well as others, said that Ichazo taught "ego fixations."[17] It is possible Ichazo was using some of the "seven deadly
sins" for the Enneagram, but the idea was to transcend the ego in
order to be liberated. As stated in a lawsuit filed in 1992 on behalf
of Arica against the psychic Helen Palmer:

> An ego fixation is an accumulation of life experience or-
> ganized during one's childhood and which shapes one's per-
> sonality. Arica training seeks to overcome the control and in-
> fluence of the ego fixations so that the individual may return to
> the inner balance with which he or she was born.[18]

In this paradigm held by Ichazo's Arica Institute, one's "true
self" is divine and perfect; but through confusion caused by wrong
beliefs, one has allegedly identified with the ego which is termed
the "false self." Subsequently, there is the "true self" versus the
"false self," a concept familiar to anyone who has studied Eastern

religions, Gnosticism, or New Age teachings. The Enneagram Institute, founded in 1997 by Don Richard Riso and current President Russ Hudson in Stone Ridge, New York, claims that the Enneagram will uncover the wrong view of self and lead one to realize the "true self."

> The Passions represent an underlying emotional response to reality created by the loss of contact with our Essential nature, with the ground of our Being, with our true identity as Spirit or Essence.[19]

This is but a small step from the serpent's voice in the Garden of Eden saying, *"You shall be as God"* (Genesis 3:5) to "you have forgotten you *are* god." Once you follow the path of the Enneagram, you can shed the false identity and embrace your true, *divine* identity!

How did Oscar Ichazo arrive at his new understanding of the self? Was it through careful research and testing? No. He was involved in psychedelic drugs and shamanism,[20] and asserted he had "received instructions from a higher entity called Metatron" and his Arica group "was guided by an interior master."[21]

In a 2010 video, Ichazo's student, Claudio Naranjo, states that Ichazo told him that he received the information on the ego fixations from a:

> higher source, not a historical source … from inspiration, from revelation, and that is his word,

and Naranjo says: "I trust it".[22]

In the same video, Naranjo, who is credited with revealing the Enneagram's personality types, adds that he (Naranjo) received most of the information for the types via "automatic writing."[23] Automatic writing is a form of spirit contact in which one opens up to a channel of communication from a supernatural source by allowing the source to move the hand and/or dictate the words (this can also be done with a typewriter or computer). It is not surprising that Naranjo, as one who engaged in other forms of esoteric and occult practices, would seek or have such experiences.

Ichazo's student Naranjo took the Enneagram teachings to Es-alen Institute around 1971. Esalen in Big Sur, California was and, to some degree, still is an edgy, humanistic, New Age think tank. Esalen is characterized by Dr. Ronald V. Huggins as

> a place where people were likely to get naked, take LSD, and beat on native drums.[24]

Naranjo passed on the Enneagram teachings to Roman Cath-olic Jesuit Priest Bob Ochs (1930-2018).[25] Bob Ochs took it to a seminary in Chicago where it was taught to Roman Catholics in the 1970s. Two of the then 20-something-year-old students who learned it were Roman Catholic Franciscan Priest Richard Rohr and Roman Catholic Jesuit Priest Mitch Pacwa. Richard Rohr and Mitch Pacwa eventually went in decidedly different directions. Richard Rohr went on to become perhaps the biggest recruiter for and "master teacher" of the Enneagram. After 20-plus years, Mitch Pacwa abandoned it. Becoming concerned about the Enneagram and other New Age beliefs and practices filtering into Catholicism, a 20-year older and more astute Pacwa, to his credit, in 1992, wrote *Catholics and the New Age: How Good People Are Being Drawn into Jungian Psychology, the Enneagram, and the Age of Aquarius* in 1992, which exposed these false ideas. He describes his own ex-perience learning and using it, and explains to the reader the process by which the conviction of the Scriptures led him to abandon the Enneagram. He explains:

> A number of times I was certain about having pegged my friends' enneagram types, but when they looked at their charts, they chose something different. Sometimes I found myself forcing experiences into the categories of my enneagram or limiting personal criticism of those categories, even though people saw other faults in me. It was hard to accept faults that were not part of the Enneagram descriptions.
>
> Furthermore, I became increasingly suspicious about the antiquity of the enneagram and typing personalities when I failed to find it mentioned in any books by Gurdjieff or his disciples. The enneagram figure was there, but the personality types were never mentioned. Admittedly, it was supposed to

be secret knowledge, but Gurdjieff's disciples apparently had no difficulty in revealing other sacred parts of the teaching and work in their books. Why was there no mention of it?

I gradually stopped consulting my Enneagram notes and, like many of my Jesuit friends, ignored the whole thing. Only recently has my interest been rekindled as I have seen the enneagram grow in popularity among Catholics. But my interest has become a matter of serious personal concern because of the scientific questions, social problems, and theological problems the enneagram poses for Catholics and other Christians.[26]

In Pacwa's chapter on the "Occult Roots of the Enneagram," he issues a warning:

> a conversation with Dorothy Ranaghan [(1942-), co-founder, Catholic People of Praise] and reading her booklet, *A Closer Look at the Enneagram* forced me to reconsider the possibility that there is an occult background to the enneagram. The books by Gurdjieff's disciples and articles about Oscar Ichazo prove they practiced occultism and that occultism is interwoven with the enneagram itself. Therefore, I believe Christians need to be aware of the enneagram's occult origins so they can prevent occult traces from infecting their faith in Christ Jesus.[27]

Even though at that point in time, the Enneagram had been relegated to Gnostics, mystics, occultists, and, to a certain degree, some within the Roman Catholic Church, it had not yet been noticed by evangelicals; and with concerns at the time about the growth of New Age philosophies and teachings in culture, it would not have been embraced. Even so, in an attempt to warn evangelicals away from these New Age, mystical beliefs, the Christian Research Institute (CRI) published an article in their Fall 1991 *CRI Journal*: "Tell Me Who I Am, O Enneagram" by Mitch Pacwa.[28]

Meanwhile, Naranjo's teachings made their way to New Age spiritual seekers like the psychic Helen Palmer, who began teaching and writing on the Enneagram in the 1980s. The Enneagram teachings spread throughout the New Age Movement, whose practitioners added various spiritual layers and meanings to it in the typical manner of New Age esoterics. Psychic Helen Palmer and Dr. David Daniels (1934-2017), a New Age spiritual seeker, created what is called the "Narrative Tradition" to the Enneagram in 1988. Although Daniels was a professor of psychiatry at Stanford University, he first learned the Enneagram under the teaching of New Ager Helen Palmer and came to believe in it.[29]

Richard Rohr—who had learned the Enneagram from Jesuits like Bob Ochs and Munich, Germany's St. Luke's Pastor Andreas Ebert—wrote a book on the Enneagram titled *Discovering the Enneagram: An Ancient Tool for a New Spiritual Journey,* which was published first in German in 1989. It was translated into English by Peter Heinegg and published in 1990 by Crossroad Publishing Company, New York. It is a combination of this 1990 book and the Emergent/Progressive Movement leaders' embrace of Richard Rohr which has facilitated the entrance of the Enneagram teachings into evangelical churches.

CHAPTER 5

Richard Rohr:
Which God Does He Serve?

*A*nd Elijah came near to all the people and said, "How
long will you go limping between two different opinions?
If the LORD is God, follow him; but if Baal, then follow him."
And the people did not answer him a word. (1 Kings 18:21)

Ahab was the king of Israel (B.C. 869-850). He married Jezebel
and "allowed Jezebel to sustain the cult of Baal and built a temple
to him in Samaria."[1] In 1 Kings 18, Elijah forthrightly asked the
people to choose which God (or god) would have their full alle-
giance and to stop waffling back and forth between the worship of
the true God and idolatry. Would they finally be completely loyal to
the God Who had revealed Himself in history and Scripture to His
people, or would they serve the false god Baal? Elijah wouldn't tolerate equivocation on this point. The people must choose one or the
other, but they couldn't have both, nor syncretize the two opposing
allegiances into one belief system.

Richard Rohr played a key role in bringing in and populariz-
ing the Enneagram in the evangelical churches. Therefore, it be-
hooves believers to ask the question: Is the god that Rohr presents

to Christians, the God of history and Scripture—indeed, the God of the Christian faith—or another deity? As we address this question, we must point out that this chapter is not an attempt to give a detailed view of Rohr's life, writings, or social policies. Our focus is on his theology, particularly as expressed on his website and in his book *The Universal Christ* (2019), since Rohr's teachings in his book are connected to the terms he applies to the Enneagram.[2]

Rohr is a Franciscan friar who started the Center for Action and Contemplation (CAC) in Albuquerque, New Mexico in 1986. His use of the term "Action" refers to Rohr's view of social action to bring about what he views as social justice; and the term "Contemplation" refers to contemplative practices in prayer and meditation, which he has stated is *the way* to alter one's thinking and become more "nondual." *Nonduality* refers to seeing reality as one unified whole with no distinctions, i.e., no saved/unsaved dichotomy or saying certain lifestyles are wrong while affirming others as right.[3]

Rohr's earlier book with Andreas Ebert, *Discovering the Enneagram,* was released in 1992 (trans. Peter Heinegg; New York: Crossroad, 1992). A book in the German language had been published in 1989 and a translation of that, *Discovering the Enneagram: An Ancient Tool for a New Spiritual Journey* (Crossroad Publishing Company, New York) first came out in 1990. *The Enneagram: A Christian Perspective* (2018) is a revised and expanded edition of the German publication.

In the preface to that book, Richard Rohr calls the Enneagram:

> a very ancient Christian tool for the discernment of spirits, for the struggle with our capital sin, our 'False Self,' and the encounter with our True Self in God.[4]

But are they referring to God as found in Scripture or some other? Ebert writes in the 1992 introduction to Richard Rohr and Andreas Ebert, *Discovering the Enneagram: An Ancient Tool for a New Spiritual Journey*:

The Enneagram is a mysterious model of the psyche that

is not originally Christian.[5]

I believe that the Enneagram can help us to find a deeper and more authentic relationship with God—even though it was not discovered by Christians.[6]

Rohr asserts that the Enneagram is:

another one of the endlessly brandished swords of the Holy Spirit,

and that the Enneagram is:

like the Spirit of truth, will always set you free.[7]

Without even knowing Rohr's theology, someone who is biblically literate should see problems with these claims. First of all, as we have already demonstrated earlier in this book (see chapter 3), the Enneagram is *neither ancient nor Christian*. Secondly, it is hardly "one of the ... swords of the Holy Spirit." Scripture defines what the sword of the Spirit is, and the work it does:

the sword of the Spirit, which is the word of God. (Ephesians 6:17)

For the word of God is living and active, sharper than any two-edged sword, piercing to the division of soul and of spirit, of joints and of marrow, and discerning the thoughts and intentions of the heart. (Hebrews 4:12)

The Enneagram also is neither "like the Spirit of truth," nor is it able to "set you free." It is Christ alone who sets free all who believe in Him (John 8:36; Acts 13:39; Romans 7:24-25; Galatians 5:1). These claims demonstrate a vastly diminished knowledge of Scripture. The comparison of a recent, manmade tool from the occult and the New Age to the Holy Spirit is a disquieting glimpse into how Rohr's Enneagram teachings are riddled with theological problems.

Creation and Panentheism

Rohr teaches that creation was the first Incarnation of Christ.[8] On his website, Rohr writes:

> God spoke the Eternal Blueprint/Idea called *Christ,* "and so it was!" (Genesis 1:9). Two thousand years ago marks the Incarnation of God in Jesus, but before that there was the Incarnation through light, water, land, sun, moon, stars, plants, trees, fruit, birds, serpents, cattle, fish, and "every kind of wild beast" according to the Genesis creation [sic] story (Genesis 1:3-25). This is the "Cosmic Christ" through which God has "let us know the mystery of God's purpose, the hidden plan made from the beginning *in Christ"* (Ephesians 1:9-10).[9]

The first Incarnation of Christ was creation itself, according to Rohr. So, all creation (including human beings) is in Christ and everyone and everything has "divine DNA."[10] Since everyone is in Christ already, there is no need for salvation. Christ is "another name for everything."[11] His assertions reveal Rohr is decidedly heretical in his understanding and teaching on the nature of salvation.

When it comes to the nature of God, Rohr openly admits to being a panentheist, and it is central to his belief system. *Panentheism* is *the belief that God is in creation as our essence is in our body. Creation is in God Who is more than all elements of creation added together.*[12] It is not *pantheism,* which is *the belief that God equals creation.*[13] Panentheism is found in neo-orthodoxy, Progressive Christianity, the New Age, mysticism, and Eastern Orthodoxy (their view involves God having "essence" and "energies").

Since Rohr teaches that the first Incarnation of Christ was creation, then Christ is literally *in* creation. He explains:

> God is not just saving people; God is saving all of creation. It is all "Real Presence." We could call it the primordial "Christification" or anointing of the universe at Creation. This is not pantheism (God is everything), but pan*en*theism (God is *in* everything!). [14]

Christ is the eternal amalgam of matter and spirit as one.

They hold and reveal one another. Wherever the human and
the divine coexist, we have the Christ. Wherever the material and the spiritual coincide, we have the Christ. That includes the material world, the natural world, the animal world
(including humans), and moves all the way to the elemental
world [15]

Rohr expands the biblical teaching of the Incarnation—that Jesus is both divine and human—to include all creation with Christ
representing a combination of spirit and matter as one throughout
the universe. Christ is *literally* in everything, every animal, every
human, every plant, etc.

Rohr falsely claims when Paul uses the phrase *"in Christ"* in
his epistles, he means it literally—so all are in Christ. There has
never been separation from God,[16] and no salvation is needed. However, Paul is referring to the Christian *positionally* being in Christ,
united by faith with Christ. Other texts (Colossians 3:11; 1 Corinthians 15:28) are taken out of context by Rohr in an attempt to support
his view; but if one reads these passages in context and in light of
the rest of Scripture, it is evident they do not support panentheism.[17]

Panentheism alters the nature of God, because it makes God
subject to creation and puts Him in time. This means God is contin-
gent (dependent) and not immutable. Immutability is a classic attribute of God, meaning God does not change or react to time or other
forces. God is neither vulnerable to anything, nor does He react;
because that would mean He is unpredictable, and could change for
better or worse, which would mean He is not perfect. It also would
mean He is not omniscient, because He could change His mind.

The Bible

Rohr weighs in on his view of Scripture in his comments about
the Bible:

> The Bible is an anthology of many books. It is a record
> of *people's experience of God's self-revelation.* It is an account of
> our very human experience of the divine intrusion into history.
> The book did not fall from heaven in a pretty package. It was
> written by people trying to listen to God. I believe that the

Spirit was guiding the listening and writing process. We must also know that humans always see "through a glass darkly ... and all knowledge is imperfect." (1 Corinthians 13:12).[18]

Rohr views the Bible as a collection of books that merely record the authors' experience of God or convey who they thought God was. The Bible is not viewed as God's revelation. Rohr states:

Just as the Bible takes us through many stages of consciousness and history, it takes us individually a long time to move beyond our need to be dualistic, judgmental, accusatory, fearful, blaming, egocentric, and earning—and to see as Jesus sees.[19]

Rohr believes the Bible reveals men's thoughts at different "stages of consciousness." He refers to Ken Wilber's (1949-) theory of "Spiral Dynamics®" of colors to explain this.[20] (Ken Wilber writes on transpersonal psychology and something he developed which he calls "Integral Theory.")

Sin, Atonement, Resurrection, and Salvation

Rohr undermines the concept of sin and redefines it, saying the only real sin is thinking we are separate from God. In his book *The Universal Christ*, Rohr scoffs at Adam's sin being "a single sin committed between the Tigris and Euphrates rivers" as though it is of no account.[21]

Since sin as defined by God is rejected by Rohr, that means the cross was not God's judgment on sin, but rather "God's great act of solidarity" with everyone and everything in creation; it is "a statement from God that *reality has a cruciform pattern*."[22]

Rohr argues that "salvation is not a question of if but when."[23] Rohr believes everything and everyone will be swept into the final point of perfection, drawn to that end by Christ.

"All who look at the world with respect," writes Rohr, "even if they are not formally religious, are en Cristo, or in Christ."[24]

In a 2009 interview, Rohr stated, "Incarnation is already redemption. Bethlehem was more important than Calvary."[25] Rohr believes the Incarnation of Jesus was bringing the "Universal Christ" into form so that this Christ could be unleashed at the Resurrection and pull everyone and everything to redemption. He said this in the same interview:

> <u>Resurrection</u> fits into this shift in point of view beautifully and necessarily. <u>Jesus died, Christ arose.</u> That's precisely what the transformation is—Christ's consciousness untied from a specific place and time.
>
> When I was studying systematic theology back in the 1960s, my professor put it this way: If a video camera had been present at the moment of Jesus' resurrection, we would not have seen a body leaving the tomb but probably a vast flash of light as that limited human body that contained Jesus became identified with something beyond space and time. It's a way to understand the Resurrection. That's why you and I have access to Christ. It's why Jesus can say he is with us until the end of time and available everywhere. You can see the New Testament's Resurrection stories saying precisely that. The angel asked, "Why are you looking up to the heavens for him?"[26]

Rohr takes the angel's question out of context. Actually, Acts records *two angels* being present. They were not saying the Universal Christ was now everywhere, but rather that Jesus had been taken *"into heaven,"* and that Jesus will return *"just the same way."*

> *They also said, "Men of Galilee, why do you stand looking into the sky? This Jesus, who has been taken up from you into heaven, will come in just the same way as you have watched Him go into heaven."* (Acts 1:11)

Not surprisingly, the return of Jesus at the Second Coming is likewise given a different slant by Rohr, who ties it to his belief Jesus already indwells creation:

> We're all unworthy but the mystery of the Incarnation means the divine indwelling is in all of us. We're indeed the body of Christ. God's hope for humanity is that one day we will all recognize that the divine dwelling place is

all of creation. <u>Christ comes again whenever we see that matter and spirit coexist.</u> This truly deserves to be called good news.[27]

According to Rohr, the Second Coming simply turns into a future realization by all that Christ is already a part of creation.

In chapter 13 of his book, Rohr reads "universal salvation" into passages like Romans 8:3, Hebrews 2:19, Hebrews 7:28, Philippians 3:9-12, and Philippians 3:21. He believes the original message of Jesus was a *universal salvation,* and that the church later turned it into *individualized salvation* due to dualistic thinking, which he repeatedly denounces.

Jesus/Christ

Perhaps the most egregious heresy from Rohr is a distinction between Jesus and Christ. He agrees Jesus is the Son of God, was born of a virgin, and had deity. But he explains Jesus and Christ are *two distinct beings:*

> Jesus is a map for the time-bound and personal level of life; Christ is the blueprint for all time and space and life itself. Both reveal the universal pattern of self-emptying and infilling (Christ) and death and resurrection (Jesus), which is the process humans have called "holiness," "salvation," or "growth."[28]

Even back in 2009, Rohr was teaching a distinction between Jesus and Christ:

> The Gospels are about the historical Jesus. Paul, however, whose writings make up a third of the New Testament, never talks about that Jesus. He is talking about the Christ. Jesus is the microcosm; Christ is the macrocosm. There is a movement between the two that we ourselves have to imitate in our life and walk, the resurrection journey.[29]

Rohr's Jesus is always portrayed as more limited, as though He was merely the one who carried this "Universal Christ" in His being.

Christ is eternal; Jesus is born in time. Jesus without Christ invariably becomes a time-bound and culturally-bound religion that excludes much of humanity from Christ's embrace. On the other end, Christ without Jesus would easily become an abstract metaphysics or a mere ideology without personal engagement. We must believe in Jesus *and* Christ.[30]

The "Christ" Rohr presents is allegedly "older" and "larger" than Jesus. Rohr continually refers to the mystics and the "Eastern Fathers" as having understood this distinction, while others did not. However, historic Christianity *never* adopted panentheism.

But it seems we so fell in love with this personal interface in Jesus that we forgot about the eternal Christ, the Body of God, which is all of creation, which is really the "First Bible." Jesus and Christ are not exactly the same. In the early Christian era, only a few Eastern Fathers (such as Origen of Alexandria and Maximus the Confessor) noticed that the Christ was clearly historically older, larger, and different than Jesus himself.[31]

After the Resurrection (as defined by Rohr), the "Universal Christ" emerged and allowed the body of Jesus to move "beyond all limits of space and time into a new notion of physicality and light —which includes all of us in its embodiment."[32] Rohr's distinction between Jesus and his idea of the "Universal Christ" is evident. Rohr's kind of resurrection puts all of us into his "Universal Christ." This renders the crucifixion of Jesus Christ as impotent!

Rohr claims the "Universal Christ" is speaking in John 14:6, and says he is the way for everyone, because everyone is part of creation.

Jesus gives us *his risen presence* as "the way, the truth, and the life" (John 14:6). No dogma will ever substitute for that.[33]

we made Jesus Christ into an exclusive savior instead of the totally inclusive savior he was meant to be. As my friend Brian McLaren likes to put it, "Jesus is the Way—he's not standing in the way!"[34]

In his footnote, Rohr points readers to an article regarding John 14:6 by post-modern pastor, author, and emergent church leader Brian McLaren (1956-), in which McLaren attempts to persuade readers that Jesus was not saying He is the only way to God.

Rohr gives a vivid illustration that reveals his distinction between Jesus and the "Universal Christ:"

> If Christ is the kite, Jesus is the person flying the kite and keeping it from escaping away into invisibility.
>
> If Jesus is the person holding the string, Christ is the great banner in the sky, from whom all can draw life—even if they do not recognize the one flying the kite.
>
> Jesus does not hold the kite to himself as much as he flies it aloft, for all to see and enjoy.[35]

To summarize Rohr's distinction between Jesus and his Universal Christ: Jesus is holding the kite, which is the Universal Christ, so that all can see this Christ even if they don't see or know Jesus.

Perennialism

Rohr also admits to being a Perennialist. *Perennialism* is *the belief that there is one Divine Reality at the center of all religions.* From Rohr's site:

> The Perennial Tradition encompasses the recurring themes in all of the world's religions and philosophies that continue to say:
> - There is a Divine Reality underneath and inherent in the world of things,
> - There is in the human soul a natural capacity, similarity, and longing for this Divine Reality, and
> - The final goal of existence is union with this Divine Reality.[36]

Because of his Perennialist beliefs, Rohr accepts that the beliefs in Buddhism, the New Age, Hinduism, Islam, or any religion are valid. Whatever differences there appear to be among religions, Rohr believes they share a common essence, a "Divine Reality," and all paths end in the same truth.

Panentheism and perennialism both lead Rohr to the false conclusions that no one needs any kind of salvation; all are "in" Christ
already; all religions share the same core truth; and all that is needed
is for people to realize these ideas.

Dualism, Nondualism, and Contemplation

Rohr commonly asserts that we need to move from a dual mind-
set (making or discerning distinctions) to one that is non-dual (not
making or discerning distinctions). Rohr accepts dualism for practical things like doing math or learning to drive, but he associates
dualism with judgment and condemnation in a spiritual context. For
Rohr, a change in consciousness is needed as part of the "Emerging" (Progressive) Christianity:

> What is happening in Emerging Christianity is far bigger
> than any mere structural or organizational re-arrangement. It is
> a revolutionary change in Christian consciousness itself. It is a
> change of mind and of heart that has been a long time in com-
> ing and now seems to be a new work of the Holy Spirit. Only
> such a sea-change of consciousness—drawing from the depths
> of the Great Ocean of Love—will bear fruits that will last.
> The change that changes everything is the movement away
> from dualistic thinking toward non-dual consciousness. We
> know that if we settle for our old patterns of dualistic thought,
> this emerging phenomenon will be just one more of the many
> reformations in Christianity that have characterized our entire
> history. The movement will quickly and surely subdivide into
> liberal or conservative, Catholic or Protestant, intellectual or
> emotional, gay or straight, liturgical or Pentecostal, feminist
> or patriarchal, activist or contemplative—like all of the other
> dualisms—instead of the wonderful holism of Jesus, a fully
> contemplative way of being active and involved in our suffer-
> ing world.[37]

Rohr equates "dualistic thinking" with division and strife. Cate-
gorizing people into areas of their beliefs is divisive and destructive
in Rohr's view. Therefore, he teaches we need to move to a new,
"non-dual consciousness." One way this is to come about is through

what Rohr terms "contemplation."

Rohr's organization is called the Center for Action and Contemplation (CAC) for a reason. He is a strong advocate of contemplation, which he terms "Christian." However, his definition of it and how he views its purpose is not in line with the biblical meaning. Biblically, meditation is on the Word of God and on God and what He has done (for example: Joshua 1:8; Psalm 1:2; Psalm 63:6; Psalm 77:12).

> Contemplative prayer, remaining silently and openly in God's presence, "rewires" our brains to think non-dually with compassion, kindness, and a lack of attachment to the ego's preferences.
>
> In contemplative prayer we move beyond language to experience God as Mystery. We let go of our need to judge, defend, or evaluate, plugging into the mind of Christ which welcomes paradox and knows its true identity in God.
>
> During contemplation we come to know that there is no separation between sacred and secular. All is one with Divine Reality.[38]

For Rohr, contemplation is the method to bring one to the realization that he or she is already "in" Christ, and to the non-dualistic understanding that all is "one" with what he calls "Divine Reality" (seemingly, his term for God). Rohr is, therefore, a passionate advocate of contemplative practices, including Contemplative Prayer. This type of prayer is not normative prayer as found in Scripture, but rather, it is a certain method that is more akin to Eastern meditation techniques.[39]

Rohr frequently refers with admiration to the late Catholic Monk and Trappist Priest Thomas Keating (1923-2018) who, along with two others, founded the modern Contemplative Prayer Movement.

Rohr believes contemplation "rewires our brain" and induces an understanding of non-dual reality. In a video posted on January 10, 2019 on Contemplative Prayer, Rohr redefines prayer, claims Jesus practiced Contemplative Prayer, and says that Contemplative Prayer is "a different form of consciousness."[40]

These and other heretical beliefs of Rohr's are being spread through the Enneagram teachings and other venues, which are addressed in the next chapter.

If Rohr's teachings are true, we must abandon what the historic Christian church has taught and maintained since its inception. If they are false, Richard Rohr must be exposed as a false teacher, and the occult "spiritual tool" called the Enneagram must be abandoned. Today, as in the days of Elijah, the people must choose whom they will serve.

CHAPTER 6

Reap the Whirlwind

Set the trumpet to your lips! One like a vulture is over the house of the LORD, because they have transgressed my covenant and rebelled against my law. To me they cry, "My God, we—Israel—know you." Israel has spurned the good; the enemy shall pursue him.

They made kings, but not through me. They set up princes, but I knew it not. With their silver and gold they made idols for their own destruction. I have spurned your calf, O Samaria. My anger burns against them. How long will they be incapable of innocence? For it is from Israel; a craftsman made it; it is not God. The calf of Samaria shall be broken to pieces.

For they sow the wind, and they shall reap the whirlwind.
(Hosea 8:1-7a)

The issue of embracing false teachings, false teachers, false prophets, and unfaithful leaders permeates all of the history of the people of God. It began in Genesis, flows through the history and lineage of the Nation of Israel, and has subverted and twisted the teachings of the church—the body of Christ—to various degrees from its inception. As Hosea reveals, ancient Israel had not engaged in an overt denial of God. They claimed to *know* God. *"My God, we—Israel—know you"* (Hosea 8:2). Although they continued to speak the *language of faith,* they had *redefined the terms.* They had turned to a manmade faith and practice in spite of God's explicitly commanding them not to do so. The leaders and priests allowed, even encouraged, false teachers to pass on false teachings and practices to their acolytes who, in turn, passed it on to the nation. The people of God again forgot their God and discarded the true faith in favor of *"everyone doing what is right in their own eyes"* (cf. Deuteronomy 12:1-8); and they ended up bereft of God and all that really matters.

Spurning God

When one examines Richard Rohr's disturbing and heretical theology, one discovers he redefines historic, foundational, biblical terms: Christ, sin, redemption, and man among other things. Our conclusions are not based upon the fact we are Evangelicals and Rohr is Roman Catholic. It is also the results of research and findings of the Roman Catholic apologetics group Catholic Answers as summed up in their article "A Primer on Richard Rohr:"

> The Christ whom Rohr preaches is not the authentic Jesus, and his related proclamation of the gospel [sic] is not the one that that [sic] the Church has proclaimed and safeguarded for 2,000 years with the power of Holy Spirit. As a result, Rohr remains an unreliable and spiritually dangerous guide for Catholic and non-Catholic alike.[1]

Rohr has deeply invested himself in discipling others and teaching his acolytes to spread his alternative gospel—*"another gospel"* and *"another Jesus"* (cf. 2 Corinthians 11:4). As one reads his material and notes his definitions of the theology which he is promoting and handing down to his evangelists, one should not be astonished to see his influence on the Enneagram teachings now permeating the evangelical churches.

The authors of two popular Enneagram books used by Evangelicals—Christopher L. Heuertz *(The Sacred Enneagram)* and

Ian Cron and Suzanne Stabile *(The Road Back to You)*—were mentored by Richard Rohr.[2] Rohr authored the foreword to Heuertz's volume. There are other connections that indicate a collaboration of views and mutual support. Rohr is on the Board of Gravity: A Center for Contemplative Activism, an organization co-founded and run by Chris Heuertz and his wife, Phileena.[3] Phileena Heuertz is on the Executive and Nominations Committees of Rohr's Center for Action and Contemplation (CAC).[4]

As noted earlier, Heuertz has echoed Rohr's incorrect teachings on the Enneagram's origins as being ancient and Christian. This false information has been repeated countless times by other Christian Enneagram teachers,[5] which sadly leads their followers to false gods and into false practices.

In a promotion for a 2019 *Workbook* as a companion guide to Heuertz's book *The Sacred Enneagram,* Zondervan—which is a publisher that is generally trusted in evangelical circles—mentions Heuertz "has been influenced by work of Rohr and other Enneagram experts such as Helen Palmer, and Russ Hudson, as well as contemplative spirituality teachers such as Jean Vanier, Henri Nouwen and Thomas Keating" as though all of these teachers are commendable and help to establish credibility.[6] What Zondervan either doesn't know or fails to mention is that both Palmer and Hudson are New Agers.

God and Jesus in the Enneagram

During an interview with Ian Cron and Suzanne Stabile, co-authors of *The Road Back to You*, they were asked what Enneagram number Jesus was. Their response:

> Jesus represents all numbers; it has been said in Christian Enneagram tradition that <u>the Enneagram is the face of God.</u> If you read the Gospels and you're Enneagram literate, you'll find that Jesus has stories specifically addressing each of the nine ways of seeing the world.[7]

It should be noted Suzanne Stabile was mentored for several years by Richard Rohr,[8] and both Cron and Stabile teach at Rohr's Center for Action and Contemplation (CAC).[9]

The Enneagram teacher Bill Gaultiere (1963?-), Ph.D., is described in his bio at Christian Soul Care as "a licensed Psychologist (PSY12036 in CA), certified Spiritual Director, and ordained Pastor."[10] At the organization he and his wife Kristi[11] co-cofounded, Soul Shepherding Institute in Irvine, CA,[12] his bio adds "pastor/mentor to pastors."[13] He states in his Enneagram presentation[14] at Saddleback Community Church:

> at <u>the center of the Enneagram is our Lord Jesus Christ</u>. He is the perfection of all nine types; they integrate in Him.

Gaultiere added:

> When you see Jesus in the Enneagram, you see who you are meant to be.[15]

Promoting the Enneagram as a picture of "the face of God" is not only inaccurate, but also is a deeply misleading tactic which attempts to make the Enneagram seem biblical. Is this a repeat of the practices for which God called ancient Israel to task? They were claiming to *know* God while pointing to an image of human creation as being God. How is this any different from Israel creating a golden calf ... not once, but twice ... to represent the only true God: YHWH? [God's Hebrew name *YHWH* is translated *LORD* in English.] In Exodus 32:4, Aaron created a golden calf and built an altar before it to sacrifice to the calf as to YHWH (Exodus 32:5-6). King Jeroboam doubled down and created two golden calves as representations of YHWH (1 Kings 12: 28-29).[16]

Gaultiere also recommends Richard Rohr twice in this video, as well as the Enneagram book written by New Agers Don Riso and Russ Hudson.[17] He calls Richard Rohr "a great Christian teacher" and "a very wise teacher."[18] He has read and re-read Rohr's book, and he thinks it is great.

Pastor Paul Taylor (1972?-) of Rivers Crossing Community Church in Ohio did a sermon series on the Enneagram. He calls the Enneagram "an ancient tool" (by way of reminder, this is untrue) and then repeats the falsehood that the Enneagram started with Evagrius Ponticus, a fourth-century monk. Around the 11:30 mark of the online video, he talks about meeting Enneagram author Ian Morgan Cron, who is co-author of *The Road Back to You.* Cron endorses and admires Richard Rohr as well as Beatrice Chestnut, a New Age psychotherapist.[19]

A series of sermons on each number of the Enneagram was given by Pastor Matt Brown of Sandals Church in California. He states that the series is called "You," because that's what it is about. He asserts that God "wants to enhance the beauty that is in you" and "heal the brokenness." Learning the Enneagram will supposedly aid people in this and bring about "transformation." Moreover, Pastor Brown says his church will use the Enneagram "as a tool to help God teach you about yourself."[20]

Brown is presenting the Enneagram as a tool for transformation and a way to either learn how God can enhance what is already in you, or as the tool that will bring it about. This is a substitution for God's Word—the Bible—as the source of information about who we are, and how we grow in Christ. It also could lead to a default reliance on the Enneagram rather than on the power of the Holy Spirit in the life of the Christian.

False Self/True Self

The language of "false self" and "true self" was used by Roman Catholic Trappist Monk Thomas Merton (1915-1968), whom Rohr considers to be a mentor.[21] Rohr asserts that,

> The <u>False Self</u> is simply a substitute for our deeper and deepest truth. It is a useful and even needed part of ourselves, but it is not all; the danger is when we think we are only our false, separate, small self. Our attachment to False Self must die to allow <u>True Self</u>—our basic and unchangeable identity in God—to live fully and freely.[22]

What Rohr means is the "False Self" is the incorrect belief that we are separate from God. Since, as Rohr teaches it, Christ incarnated as creation, then all are in Christ and in God and, therefore, never separate. The "True Self" is literally "in" God in Rohr's view. This forms the crux of his teaching that the Enneagram helps one to discover this "True Self."

Rohr laments that people don't realize the core of their being is a pure, untouched essence, stating that in:

> the depths of their hearts where neither sin nor desire nor
> self-knowledge can reach, the core of their reality, [is] the per-
> son that each one is in God's eyes.[23]

He expands on this, explaining all people have a part within
"untouched by sin."

> At the center of our being is a point of nothingness which
> is <u>untouched by sin</u> and by illusion, a point of pure truth, a
> point or spark which belongs entirely to God, which is never
> at our disposal, from which God disposes of our lives, which
> is inaccessible to the fantasies of our own mind or the bru-
> talities of our own will. This little point of nothingness and of
> absolute poverty is the pure glory of God in us. …. It is like a
> <u>pure diamond,</u> blazing with the invisible light of heaven. It is
> in everybody [24]

This "pure diamond" is the *essence* or "True Self" Rohr
wants people to realize. This was a theme of his book *Immortal
Diamond.*[25] However, God tells us that *"all have sinned"* (Romans 3:23) and are utterly without hope unless one has put one's
faith in Jesus Christ (Romans 4:5, Romans 4:24-25). God's Word
tells us that even our *"righteous deeds"* are as a *"filthy garment"*
(Isaiah 64:6).

Rohr uses his distinction between Jesus and Christ as a model
for moving from the "false self" to "the Christ consciousness," as
stated here:

> The Incarnation means the divine indwelling is not out
> there, over there. It happens within us. This movement from
> Jesus to the Christ means that the same anointing that was given
> to Jesus is given to all of us. That's why he didn't say, "Worship
> me." He said, "Follow me." We've projected more onto Jesus
> than he ever asked for.
>
> Also, Jesus didn't move from Jesus to the Christ without
> death and resurrection. And we ourselves don't move from our
> independent, historical body to the <u>Christ consciousness</u> with-
> out dying to our <u>false self.</u> We, like Jesus himself, have to let
> go of who we think we are, and who we think we need to be.[26]

The "false self" is a concept used repeatedly by Rohr and forms a central purpose of the Enneagram: to uncover this "false self" and realize or awaken to the "true self." This is what Rohr terms "Christ consciousness."[27]

The "False Self/True Self" concept is carried on by Rohr's students who authored the Enneagram books most used in evangelical churches: Christopher Heuertz, Ian Cron, and Suzanne Stabile. In Enneagram teachings, the "false self" (sometimes called the "ego") is a social construct foisted on us by others. It is a result of wrong expectations and damage, while the "true self" is the "real" essence of the person—the "authentic self" and who you are supposed to be. The "false self" is reminiscent of Ichazo's "ego fixations" based on his idea that our ego is a construct that needs to be dismantled to get to the pure essence.

In *The Road Back to You*, co-author Ian Cron writes that after initially rejecting the Enneagram, he was convinced by someone named Brother Dave to reconsider it. He does so, and he tells Brother Dave he has felt "asleep for a long time" but now is "beginning to wake up."[28] Cron tells us what it really is about when he writes in the next chapter that the purpose of the Enneagram is to "dis-identify" with limiting aspects of ourselves so that we can "be reunited with our truest and best selves" which is (here he refers to Thomas Merton) that "pure diamond, blazing with the invisible light of heaven."[29] The truth of this is that this is a New Age notion about "waking up" to a Gnostic-type "true self."

What kind of meaning can this have for a professing Christian? Rohr and other Enneagram teachers may misuse the Bible to support this teaching, but an examination of the biblical passages in context reveals this idea is *not found anywhere* in Scripture. While Colossians 3 speaks of an *"old self"* and *"new self,"* this is unlike the Enneagram teachings:

> *Do not lie to one another, since you laid aside the old self with its evil practices and have put on the new self who is being renewed to a true knowledge according to the image of the One who created him.* (Colossians 3:9-10)

This passage is about putting to death the former, unredeemed *"old self"* that was enslaved to sin (Romans 6:6, Romans 6:16,

Romans 6:18), and living a regenerated life as *"slaves of righteous-ness"* (Romans 6:18). The regenerated self is the *"new self."* A parallel passage teaches the new self *"has been created in righteousness and holiness of the truth"* (Ephesians 4:22-24). This has *nothing* to do with personality traits, identifying with specific sin patterns, or using a human-based tool to attain spiritual growth.

Rather than finding an "authentic self," the Scriptures teach Christians to yield to God's Word and the Holy Spirit and *"to be conformed to the image of His Son"* through the power of the Holy Spirit (Acts 5:29; Hebrews 5:9; Romans 8:29). If anything, it is the opposite of and in opposition to the idea found in the Enneagram's "True Self."

The *"new self"* is *"hidden with Christ"* (Colossians 3:3), not a "pure essence" or "authentic self" unearthed via the Enneagram. It is a supernatural work resulting from salvation by faith in the true Jesus Christ. The emphasis in the book of Colossians is also on the overt knowledge of Jesus Christ versus the covert knowledge offered by the early Gnostic teachers, which this epistle exposes and strongly warns against. This is significant in an ironic way, since the Enneagram resembles the Gnostic teachings in offering a special, "hidden" knowledge of a "true self."

The Enneagram's "true self" is not equivalent to the *"new creature"* who is *"in Christ"* as spoken of in 2 Corinthians 5:

> *and He died for all, so that they who live might <u>no longer live for themselves, but for Him who died and rose again on their behalf.</u> Therefore, from now on we recognize no one according to the flesh; even though we have known Christ according to the flesh, yet now we know Him in this way no longer. Therefore, if anyone is <u>in Christ,</u> he is a <u>new creature</u>; the old things passed away; behold, new things have come.* (2 Corinthians 5: 15-17)

In context, this is about Redemption, being reconciled to God through faith in Jesus Christ, and finding their new relationship with Jesus Christ through the Holy Spirit more rewarding than knowing Jesus Christ during the days of His earthly ministry. It is a result of a work *by God*, not a new perception or understanding of self we get through any manmade method or philosophy—especially a faulty, invalid one. In fact, 2 Corinthians 5:15 pointedly states that the Christian *"no longer live for themselves,"* but rather now lives for Jesus Christ—*"Him who died and rose again on their behalf."*

Every Christian is being sanctified and conformed to the image of Christ, which is a work of the Holy Spirit. The Enneagram's and Rohr's "True Self/False Self" teaching is not remotely connected to this; nor, it seems, can Rohr understand the meaning of the new self in Christ since, in practice, he implicitly rejects the Bible as God's Word, and teaches a false Christ and false salvation (as documented in chapter 5). The Enneagram's "authentic self," "true self," and Rohr's "self in God" is not the *"new self"* of the Bible. It is following after the tradition of a straying or stiff-necked Israel that God is remonstrating in Hosea, a *replacement* of what God has said.

David G. Benner

David G. Benner (1947-), Ph.D., psychologist and author of more than 30 books, is published as a Christian writer by InterVarsity Press (IVP) and Baker Publishing. His books are used in Christian educational venues. Baker describes him as:

> an internationally known depth psychologist, author, spiritual guide, and personal transformation coach who lives in Toronto, Ontario. Benner has authored or edited more than thirty books, including *Soulful Spirituality* and *Spirituality and the Awakening Self.* He lectures widely around the world and has held numerous clinical and academic appointments.[30]

Marcia Montenegro (co-author of this book) came across a quote from Benner on an alleged "Christian" Enneagram page that sounded "spiritual." However, the quote did not strike her as Christian, which aroused her curiosity, since she did not know Benner. A search led to the revealing information that Benner is a master teacher at Richard Rohr's Living School for Action and Contemplation.[31] Rohr wrote the foreword to Benner's book *Presence and Encounter: The Sacramental Possibilities of Everyday Life.*

Benner also founded and directs the Selah Center: Cascadia Living Wisdom School in Gig Harbor, Washington.[32] Benner expresses perennialism in his books[33] and interviews (which is not surprising due to his strong working relationship with Rohr),[34] and refers to the "perennial wisdom tradition" in his book *Living Wisdom*. Additionally, Benner writes that although there are distinctions among religions, they share a "common core."[35] This is the quintessential belief of perennialism.

Benner speaks of:

> tapping into the <u>inner wisdom</u> that exists at the core of our being

which brings us

> into direct contact with the <u>Spirit of Wisdom</u> that is the foundation of everything in existence.[36]

Perennialists believe that every religious belief system has wisdom and shares the same core of truth or "divine reality." Every person has an inherent "inner wisdom." Benner's reference to the "Spirit of Wisdom" appears to be one of his terms for God. In perennialism, God is discussed as though He is impersonal and is often referred to by using such terms as "Divine Reality" or, perhaps, another term Benner uses: "Ultimate Reality."

Benner also refers to "the truth of our 'Christ-self' versus the 'ego-self.'"[37] This is reminiscent of Rohr's view of an inner self "untouched by sin." Benner uses the "True Self/False Self" model though, as of this writing, Benner is not publicly connected to Enneagram teaching or belief.

Benner denies divine inspiration of the Bible, stating that it is a "human creation" and that one must draw on other "wisdom traditions" to interpret it. The Bible is only one of many spiritual legacies.[38] We would respond to this by reminding believers that Christians are told to be aware of false teachings that have "*an appearance of wisdom*" but are actually "*self-made religion*" (Colossians 2:23).

In an interview, when asked to explain what wisdom is, Benner responded:

> I would suggest that, grounded in a deep awareness of the sacredness and interconnectedness of everything in existence,

wisdom is living in alignment with the creative <u>Spirit of Wisdom</u> who <u>inhabits all of creation</u> and who <u>is our truest and deepest self.</u> Much more than information or even knowledge, wisdom is a way of living that involves every aspect of our being. It is learning to access the wellbeing and wholeness that comes through participation in God's transformational agenda of cosmic whole-making.[39]

Benner expresses panentheism,[40] which, as we have verified, is also a strong belief of Richard Rohr. The claim that the "Spirit of Wisdom" not only is in "all of creation" but is "our truest and deepest self" is *markedly* different from what God teaches us in Scripture. Namely, God created everything; and God is, therefore, distinct from everything; man is sinful and needs redemption from sin. Panentheists reject the core doctrines of Scripture and the historic Christian faith—such as the nature of man, nature of God, sin, and mankind's need for salvation—or they redefine them; and, thus, their beliefs cannot be considered Christian at all. Panentheism is, by definition, another religion.

Since Benner is a master teacher at Rohr's CAC, it should come as no surprise he holds to both panentheism and perennialism.[41] What is disturbing is that he is held in high regard in Christian circles, and his books are published as Christian books and some even are used in Christian academia.

Interestingly, another colleague of Rohr's is Episcopal Priest Cynthia Bourgeault (1947-), whose focus is on mystical, contemplative spiritualty. She is also "a founding Director of both the Contemplative Society and the Aspen Wisdom School."[42] Her school is based, in part, on the teachings of none other than G. I. Gurdjieff, creator of the original Enneagram, which, we reiterate, had absolutely no personality types.[43] (See chapter 1, point 3.)

The Enneagram and the New Age

As a Perennialist, Richard Rohr affirms "wisdom" from non-Christian beliefs. He even endorsed New Age Enneagram teacher and writer Helen Palmer and stated that she could give "Christian guidance" to people.[44] In 2009, Rohr joined with New Ager Russ Hudson at a Conference on the Enneagram in

Albuquerque, New Mexico.[45]

The Enneagram has been in the New Age since the 1980s and, until recently, the majority of Enneagram books were written by New Age authors. The Enneagram Institute—which many mistakenly believe is a secular, psychological, or even Christian organization—was founded by two New Agers, Don Riso and Russ Hudson. The Institute promotes the Enneagram from a New Age worldview.

The Institute's website has changed at least three times since 2011. Each time it appears less New Age,[46] but this does not make the Enneagram Institute secular or valid. It is possible that, as the Enneagram gained new ground in Progressive Christianity and is now enjoying what appears to be a fast-paced acceptance in evangelical Christianity, the website was altered so as not to appear too spiritually aligned with the New Age.

The Enneagram associations which certify Enneagram teachers and counselors are founded and headed primarily by New Agers. These include the International Enneagram Association (IEA), whose founders are mainly New Agers such as Theodorre Donson,[47] Russ Hudson, David Daniels, Kathy Hurley, Helen Palmer, and Don Riso.[48] Maria Beesing and Andreas Ebert are also named, but as far as we can determine, they are not New Age. Beesing is a Roman Catholic Dominican nun;[49] and Ebert is a Lutheran pastor, but he is also Richard Rohr's co-author of their Enneagram book. Their involvement does not give credibility to such an Enneagram organization, but rather, it reveals that one professing the Christian faith *can* be deceived. No matter how it is sliced and diced, an Enneagram teacher, book, or organization always leads back to the New Age.

In 2019, an Enneagram Global Summit was sponsored by the very New Age SHIFT Conference (Shaping How we Invest For Tomorrow). Most of the speakers were New Agers, such as Russ Hudson, Helen Palmer, Claudio Naranjo, Beatrice Chestnut, Katherine Fauvre, Sanra Maitri, and others; but Christian Enneagram authors Christopher Heuertz and Suzanne Stabile were also speakers (as was Cynthia Bourgeault).[50] In fact, Christopher Heuertz was the keynote speaker![51]

That Christians would join in with such a New Age entourage is more than disconcerting and gives the appearance of endorsing New Age views, since the Enneagram has been a vehicle of New

Age ideas for several decades.

The fourth Enneagram book from InterVarsity Press (IVP) offers "Gratitudes" to several people—including Evagrius Ponticus, Ignatius of Loyola, and Ramón Llull—none of whom had *anything* to do with the Enneagram, since it did not even exist before the twentieth century. Claudio Naranjo and Richard Rohr, however, are rightfully mentioned along with 13 New Agers, including Helen Palmer.[52] To find a supposed Christian book published by what is thought of as a Christian publisher thanking a heretic and 13 New Agers is jarring, to say the least.

"Enneagram Masters?"

In a promotion for Christopher Heuertz' book *The Sacred Enneagram*, Zondervan stated that Heuertz had studied under "some of the great living Enneagram masters."[53] This phrase should induce questions such as: What does it mean to be an Enneagram master? Who decides if one is an Enneagram master? Are there any *dead* Enneagram masters? The answers are easy and render this statement from Zondervan rather silly.

In 2017, when Heuertz's book came out, all known Enneagram teachers were alive (although David Daniels died that year). So, logically speaking, *all* the "Enneagram masters" had to be alive, since the Enneagram of personality only became publicly known starting in the 1980s (Naranjo taught it in the 70s but not openly). The statement makes no sense; and although sounding important, it means nothing in light of these facts, especially for Christians. Moreover, no Enneagram "master" can be "great," because the Enneagram is not valid. So, what appears to be a commendation is actually an apparent caving in to and embracing of New Age propaganda.

An "Enneagram master" is a term that has been used by New Agers only for New Age Enneagram teachers. However, Suzanne Stabile terms herself an "Enneagram Master" on her website. Stabile could be the first Christian "Enneagram Master," but there is no information on how she got this title. In fact, she is described as "an internationally recognized Enneagram Master."[54] There appear to be no objective criteria for that title, and one must wonder how Stabile came to be recognized that way and by whom.

Beth McCord (1975-) is a popular Christian Enneagram "coach" who has a thriving business called "Your Enneagram Coach." On her site, she claims she was trained "by the best Enneagram experts" and "pouring hundreds of hours into advanced certifications".

She claims to be:

> simplifying the deep truths of the Enneagram from a Biblical perspective.[55]

If McCord has been studying the Enneagram for as long as she claims, she had to have had New Age teachers, since only New Agers were teaching the Enneagram until recently (aside from Richard Rohr and some Catholics). McCord names five people on her site as her teachers. In fact, McCord uses the infamous New Age phrase, "master Enneagram teacher" as she names them: "master Enneagram teachers Helen Palmer, Russ Hudson, David Daniels, and Jessica Dibbs." (The fifth one, Katherine Fauvre, is mentioned in another statement on the same page.)[56]

McCord, when asked on a *Facebook* post to name her teachers, also named Ginger Lapid-Bogda (1946-). These are all New Age people. Hudson is the co-founder with Don Riso of the New Age, Enneagram Institute. Helen Palmer has already been discussed here and was also thanked by Christopher Heuertz for his Enneagram knowledge.

By way of reminder: From the information given thus far, it seems evident New Age beliefs and heresies have gained a foothold in the church via the Enneagram. The Enneagram authors Ian Cron and Suzanne Stabile teach at Richard Rohr's CAC; Chris Heuertz and Stabile were mentored by Rohr; various Christian Enneagram teachers recommend Richard Rohr or his book.[57] Christian publishers such as Zondervan promotes *The Sacred Enneagram*'s author Christopher Heuertz as having been taught by Richard Rohr as though it's laudable; and InterVarsity Press's (IVP) fourth Enneagram book gives "Gratitudes" to 13 New Agers. Christian Enneagram teacher Beth McCord had at least six New Age teachers; and the teachings of the Enneagram itself are derived from New Age concepts.

Concerns

As a former professional astrologer, co-author Marcia Montenegro knows how easy it is for people to categorize themselves. In astrology, it is done by identifying with and divining one's human interactions and events according to one's Zodiac sun sign, or with the "rising" sign (Zodiac sign on the Eastern horizon at birth that supposedly indicates appearance and external personality), or maybe where other heavenly bodies are located in the birth chart and their alleged connections.

There is a dangerously similar pattern with the Enneagram. Christians are identifying with their Enneagram number and maybe a number and a "wing." They also identify others by Enneagram numbers; and they even talk about their marriage in terms of the Enneagram numbers assigned themselves and their spouse. The Enneagram is completely invalid. The fact there are now so many Christians believing something that is demonstrably false and in conflict with a biblical worldview is quite disturbing. Even more disturbing is the fact many Christians are being encouraged to embrace the Enneagram by their pastors and other leaders in the church.

CHAPTER 7

As for This Moses . . .

When the people saw that Moses delayed to come down from the mountain, the people gathered themselves together to Aaron and said to him, "Up, make us gods who shall go before us. As for this <u>Moses, the man who brought us up out of the land of Egypt</u>, we do not know what has become of him." So, Aaron said to them, "Take off the rings of gold that are in the ears of your wives, your sons, and your daughters, and bring them to me." So all the people took off the rings of gold that were in their ears and brought them to Aaron. And he received the gold from their hand and fashioned it with a graving tool and made a golden calf. And they said, "These are your gods, O Israel, who brought you up out of the land of Egypt!" When Aaron saw this, he built an altar before it. And Aaron made a proclamation and said, "Tomorrow shall be a feast to the LORD." (Exodus 32:1-5)

By this time in their journey, we see the Israelites have focused on God's servant Moses as being their deliverer from Egypt when the people refer to Moses as *"the man who brought us up out of the land of Egypt."* But, a little over three-and-a-half-months earlier,

99

the nation of Israel had witnessed their miraculous deliverance from Egypt. Not only were they delivered from slavery and oppression, but the citizens of Egypt gave them material wealth to carry away as plunder just as the LORD had promised (cf. Genesis 15:14, Exodus 3:20-22). The Israelites saw the miraculous parting of the Red Sea and watched the Egyptian soldiers drown as the waters collapsed on them. Three days later, they arrived at the waters of Marah; but the water was *"bitter."* God provided a miracle at the hand of Moses, which turned the water from bitter to sweet (Exodus 15:22-25). Over the next two months, as the nation made their way to Sinai under God's protection and provision communicating with them through His servant Moses, God continued performing miracles (manna, water from the rock, defeat of the Amalekites); and at Sinai, He gave the people His commandments (Exodus 20). Just to make sure they understood what was, perhaps, of utmost importance, we read:

> *And the LORD said to Moses, "Thus you shall say to the people of Israel: 'You have seen for yourselves that I have talked with you from heaven. You shall not make gods of silver to be with me, nor shall you make for yourselves gods of gold. An altar of earth you shall make for me and sacrifice on it your burnt offerings and your peace offerings, your sheep and your oxen. In every place where I cause my name to be remembered I will come to you and bless you.* (Exodus 20:22-24)

Against a backdrop of God's very recent miracles, God reminded them that He communicated directly with His people (Exodus 20:22). He reiterated His prohibition on humanly devised and created means and instruments of adding to or replacing His prescribed way of achieving spiritual connection with Him. The reason for this prohibition is simple: *Anything* mankind can devise or create will, at best, represent a mere element of God's creation. Manmade "spiritual paths" of all kinds will *always fall short* of His majesty, glory, omnipotence, omniscience, omnipresence, etc., and those paths lead people away from Him. In his book *Bible Doctrine*, Wayne Grudem (1948-), Ph.D., Research Professor of Theology and Biblical Studies at Phoenix Seminary in Arizona, explains:

We also find that God forbids his people to think of *his very being* as similar to *anything else* in the physical creation. The second commandment (Ex. 20:4) forbids us to worship or serve "any graven image" or "likeness of anything" in heaven or earth. This is a reminder that God's being is different from everything that he has created. To think of him in terms of anything else in the created universe is to misrepresent him, to limit him, to think of him as less than he really is. Indeed, while we must say that God has made all creation so that each part reflects something of his own character, we must also affirm that to picture God as existing in a form or mode of being that is like anything else in creation is to think of God in a horribly misleading and dishonoring way.[1]

As we saw in the quote from Exodus 32, less than 45 days after God clearly and specifically had conveyed to them what they were *not* to do, they did the very thing He prohibited. While Aaron was fashioning the golden calf, the crowd proclaimed, *"These are your gods, O Israel, who brought you up out of the land of Egypt!"* (Exodus 32:4). Aaron, in what seems like an attempt to refocus the crowd's attention onto the one true God, YHWH, *"built an altar before it. And Aaron made a proclamation and said, 'Tomorrow shall be a feast to the LORD.'"* (Exodus 32:5) The *Eerdmans Companion to the Bible* comments:

> The people think not of God but of Moses as their deliverer, and their need for a visual symbol of the divine presence prompts them to ask Aaron to make gods for them (v. 1). Either fearing the crowd or having himself lost faith, Aaron complies by fashioning a young bull from the Israelites' golden jewelry and identifying it as the God who brought them out of Egypt—exactly what God prohibited in the Ten Commandments (20:4). (The bull-calf represented Baal, the storm-god and god of fertility in Canaanite religion.)[2]

Why did Aaron give in to the demands of the people? He was afraid:

And Moses said to Aaron, "What did this people do to you that you have brought such a great sin upon them?" And Aaron said, "Let not the anger of my lord burn hot. You know the people, that they are set on evil. For they said to me, 'Make us gods who shall go before us. As for this Moses, the man who brought us up out of the land of Egypt, we do not know what has become of him.' So I said to them, 'Let any who have gold take it off.' So they gave it to me, and I threw it into the fire, and out came this calf." (Exodus 32:21-24)

Aaron witnessed all of God's miracles up close and personal, so we might expect him to stand firm for the LORD's clear commands, but he did not. He was a weak leader who yielded to the desires of the people in his charge. It led to catastrophe.

Idolatry, the Rule Rather than the Exception

It is easy to look back on Israel today and excoriate them for so soon abandoning God's clear revelation to them which specifically prohibited the worship of idols. How, one wonders, could they so easily have succumbed to combining pagan worship with the worship of the One True God? There are a number of other biblical examples we could cite of such brazen disobedience to God's clear commands. The building of the Tower of Babel is one such example (cf. Genesis 11). As for Israel, time and time again, they added the worship of pagan deities to their rituals and their leadership allowed and, in some cases, *promoted* the blatant idolatry and disobedience to God's commands. Moreover, what about the church? Most of the New Testament was written to refute heresy and bad behavior which were infiltrating the church as well as to outline sound doctrine and godly living. The history of Christianity is rife with heresy invading the church, turning the flock away from sound doctrine, and leading the people back into the old paths of darkness. Numerous church leaders wrote to oppose these heresies, and convened councils to expose new and pernicious false teachings. They upheld biblical doctrine by providing further clarity as each new heresy arose in opposition to the *"faith once for all delivered to the saints"* (Jude 1:3). Even so, there always seems to be an eager market for false teaching as well as false teachers ready to fill the market demand. Is that the case with the Enneagram? The online article "The Self-Help Movement That Is Upending American Christianity" by freelance journalist Allegra Hobbs (1991-) on the Progressive website *Forge,* seems to indicate this is the case:

> Though derived from an <u>ancient wisdom tradition</u>, and <u>not explicitly Christian,</u> the Enneagram has recently found a passionate following in the Evangelical world, drawing young believers culturally <u>steeped</u> as much in <u>the self-centric spiritual practices of the secular world</u>—<u>astrology, self-care, and the wellness industry</u>—as they are in biblical teachings.
>
> The Enneagram's surge in popularity among American Christians has spawned an increased demand for resources from spiritual seekers hoping to identify and explore their personality types. In response, a thriving industry has emerged to accommodate that demand.
>
> Since 2016, Evangelical publishers have released a slew of books on the topic, and the most widely-read Christian publications have seen a whirlwind of coverage. Megachurch pastors preach the system from live-streamed pulpits, and ministers of smaller churches work it into their sermons. Christians are shelling out hundreds of dollars for sessions with professional "Enneagram coaches" to find their type and pursue self-development.[3]

Hobbs correctly states that the Enneagram is "not explicitly Christian," and she insightfully notes it is attracting those who are "steeped" in "self-centric spiritual practices of the secular world." Some of the practices Hobbs names are "astrology, self-care, the wellness industry." Have Christians who are involved with this abandoned the Bible? No. They have simply *added* a mix of secular "wisdom," occultism, and New Age with a focus on self to their understanding of the Bible and self. They seem blind to the fact that *adding to the Bible subtracts from the Bible* (cf. Deuteronomy 4:2). The result of this growing trend is the birth of an industry in which publishers, social media, and even some pastors are, wittingly or unwittingly, advancing heresies at a profitable clip. Churches and individual Christians have seemingly succumbed to something sociologist Christian Smith (1960-) and Melinda Lundquist Denton,

Assistant Professor of Sociology at Clemson, termed "Moralistic Therapeutic Deism" in the 2005 book they wrote in which they view this as a religion. They gave five characteristics:

1. A God exists who created and ordered the world and watches over human life on earth.
2. God wants people to be good, nice, and fair to each other, as taught in the Bible and by most world religions.
3. The central goal of life is to be happy and to feel good about oneself.
4. God does not need to be particularly involved in one's life except when God is needed to resolve a problem.
5. Good people go to heaven when they die.[4]

At this point, those teenagers from 2005 have now grown into adults. Is this the explanation for the focus on self, the disparagement of heaven, hell, evangelism, sin, and the welcoming acceptance of the teachings of a heretical, false teacher like Richard Rohr and his acolytes right into the church? How is it that this has happened virtually unchecked given the implicit and sometimes explicit denial of essential doctrines of the historic Christian faith? We also need to ask how it is the theological ramblings and heretical descriptions regarding the nature of God, salvation, and other essentials of the historic Christian faith get past the editors of what are considered to be premier, mainsteam, evangelical publishers? The issues and observations we are addressing are not the results of our research alone. Others like Dr. Kenneth Berding (1964-), Ph.D., Professor of New Testament at Talbot School of Theology at Biola University wrote "The Not-So-Sacred Enneagram: A Book Review of *'The Sacred Enneagram'* by Christopher L. Heuertz" in response to questions by his students. It contains very little commentary, but instead, it cites a number of direct quotes from Heuertz's book concerning the essentials of the faith which demonstrate the denial of core biblical doctrine. His conclusion was:

> Christopher Heuertz is promoting many false doctrines in his book *The Sacred Enneagram*. I write this with great grief and deep sorrow. *The Sacred Enneagram* is full of incorrect and misleading religious assertions. His teaching does not

match what the Bible communicates regarding sin, salvation, sanctification, and probably also other core doctrines such as the nature of God, the person of Jesus Christ, and the atonement. He portrays the Enneagram as sacred, powerful, searching, alive. He mixes false religious ideas together with Christianity and seems unconcerned about the Enneagram's syncretistic origins.[5]

The hunger for something other than God and His self-revelation in the Word of God has been the human condition since Adam and Eve and continues today. Like Moses' brother Aaron and the Nation of Israel, the pressure to provide *another way* to achieve a spiritual connection with God has displaced the regular, systematic, sound teaching regarding reading, reflecting on, assimilating, and living out the Word of God in many churches. Christopher Heuertz calls it "*The Sacred Enneagram.*" Is the Enneagram *sacred,* or is it today's version of the golden calf?

Unfortunately, many in church leadership believe their people read, know, and understand the Word of God. To be sure, some do. But too many do not. There is nothing inherently wrong with big churches. Yet, it does appear the larger churches of our day, in an effort to preach on issues seemingly "more relevant to people's lives today," produce a greater decline in biblical literacy amongst their ranks; although smaller churches where the emphasis is not on sound, biblical teaching are certainly not exempt. Yes, the congregation may raise a book in the air and repeat, "This is my Bible ...," but too few read, study, or meditate on it. Instead, they too often are being conditioned or taught to "go into the silence" where they can, as Richard Rohr puts it, "unlearn" the written Word of God and wait in the silence for some type of communication *apart from Scripture.* The focus moves on to what you can do for yourself and seeks ways to know God and/or yourself apart from His written revelation. Church members may affirm a church's "Doctrinal Statement," but many have little or no understanding of what it means. There is *nothing more relevant to people's lives* than the plain truths in the Word of God. But, it appears that many in leadership who are pursuing this for their congregations might just agree with the opinion of Christopher Heuertz, who suggests the present popularity of Richard Rohr and the Enneagram is due to evangelical Christians being "worn out from the same old literal Bible." The Enneagram is offering an "enhancement" to *the faith delivered once for all to the saints*" (Jude 3) or, worse, a substitute:

> I sort of wonder if <u>the evolved evangelical is getting a little worn out from the same old literal Bible</u> study interpretations of stuff. At least Catholicism can appeal to tradition and saints. I wonder if some evangelicals have gotten bored with what their tradition offers, and therefore, they find a deeper and more contemplative system like the Enneagram appealing.[6]

The problem isn't because "the evolved evangelical is getting a little worn out from the same old literal Bible study interpretations of stuff." The problem is too many Evangelicals are being "evolved" *right out of their faith* by running after the pseudo wisdom of the world and the occult. Far too few engage in serious Bible study and *biblical* meditation, which is *very different* from the mystical version of meditation being taught to them today. Too many in evangelical churches have very little, if any, grasp on the essential doctrines of the historic Christian faith. This isn't simply our opinion. In 2016, LifeWay Research conducted a survey of 3000 people[7] which demonstrates the truth of our contention with clarity. In "Survey Finds Most American Christians Are Actually Heretics," G. Shane Morris (1989-), Assistant Editor at BreakPoint/Colson Center, writes of the results of the 3000 surveyed:

> Seven out of ten respondents in LifeWay's survey affirmed the doctrine of the Trinity—that the Father, Son, and Holy Spirit are three Persons but one God, and six in ten agreed that Jesus is both human and divine. Their orthodoxy—and consistency—ended there. More than half went on to indicate that Jesus is "the first and greatest being created by God," a heresy known as Arianism, which the Council of Nicaea condemned in 325 A.D.

LifeWay Research repeated the study with 586 evangelicals as defined by the National Association of Evangelicals (NAE). Under the subheading "Evangelicals Didn't Even Study for This Test," he delivers the bad news:

Everyone expected them to perform better than most Americans. No one expected them to perform *worse*. Seven in ten evangelicals—*more than the population at large*—said that Jesus was the first being God created. Fifty-six percent agreed that "the Holy Spirit is a divine force but not a personal being." They also saw a huge increase in evangelicals (28 percent, up from 9 percent) who indicated that the Third Person of the Trinity is not equal with God the Father or Jesus, a direct contradiction of orthodox Christianity. The Holy Spirit is, of course, used to being overlooked. But sources say he seemed bummed about these results.

As before, it's really the contradictory answers, not the outright heresies, that should most concern us. By definition, the evangelicals in this survey believed that "only those who trust in Jesus Christ alone as their Savior receive God's free gift of eternal salvation." Yet nearly half agreed that "God accepts the worship of all religions including Christianity, Judaism, and Islam."

Two-thirds of evangelicals—more than Americans in general—said heaven is a place where all people will ultimately be reunited with their loved ones. That such a high percentage of Billy Graham's camp is now talking like Rob Bell isn't even the real story. The most striking thing is how many of these folks evidently see no contradiction between their casual universalism and the evangelical creed that salvation comes through faith in Christ alone.[8]

It is interesting that the incursion of the teachings of Richard Rohr and his trained Enneagram troops invaded the church through evangelical publishers in 2016—the very same year this survey demonstrated the dearth of anything approaching an orthodox view of the basic, essential doctrines of the historic Christian faith as found in the Bible.

Do-It-Yourself Spirituality

A case in point is the story of Sarajane Case (1986-), who describes herself as "writer, speaker and podcaster."[9] As she tells the story, she grew up in church, attended every Sunday, and went on to attend a "Southern Baptist university." In 2010 (at approx. 24-years old), she left Christianity and the church; and five years later, she was introduced to the Enneagram:

> Today, Case is a well-known figure in the Enneagram movement. She is comfortably situated at the top of an Enneagram online content machine that is dominated and consumed predominantly by Christians. She runs an Instagram account with a following of roughly half a million, *Enneagram and Coffee,* where she shares a mixture of insight, tips for growth, and fun memes around the constellation of types springing from the personality rubric.[10]

What led to her change in faith? As we read her story, that of Christopher Heuertz, as well as other Enneagram leaders, there is a similar tale. Heuertz writes of his case:

> Much of my elementary and secondary education growing up in Omaha, Nebraska, took place in Catholic and Protestant private schools. As a child, both at church and at school, I was taught and retaught stories from Scripture on colorful one-dimensional flannel-graph boards. There was little explicit doctrine fused into the stories (I can imagine the implicit doctrinal slants I must have ingested) until I moved into adolescence, when apologetics and theology entered my religious formation process.[11]

We are not told the depth or extent of his "apologetics and theology" training as an adolescent; and, more to the point, how much he *understood* and *retained* of that knowledge. We should also pause for a moment here and briefly acknowledge that something is sometimes missing in dealing with the growth of false teaching. The question isn't always what pastors may or may not be doing to prevent it. There is also the question of what those in their charge are hearing, retaining, and putting into practice. The teaching flows from the teacher or pastor. In turn, the students or members in the congregation hears, doesn't hear, or partially hears, and goes on to fill in the blanks themselves—mostly derived from other sources outside and inside the faith. These ideas are added to the mix, which can distort and change the original teaching in sometimes destructive ways. We can see in the stories of Case and Heuertz, they each may have had a sense of biblical doctrine but not a well-developed understanding of the essentials of the faith. For example, Heuertz implicitly denies the biblical teachings that we are born with a sin nature, and we sin by choice. He does this as he outlines his belief that humans are essentially good:

> In the incarnation [sic], when God became human, the notion that there is <u>goodness in humanity</u> was restored. And with the possibility of restoration came hope for redemption.[12]

Heuertz makes crystal clear his view that the "goodness in humanity" was always present, but we lost the notion or belief of our inherent goodness. Jesus Christ, in this scenario, incarnated to give us the ability to believe in our inherent goodness again. From there, Heuertz redefines *redemption* as *following your personal path on the Enneagram*. This will guide you to discover your original, inherent, good self—or what Enneagram teachers refer to as the "true self." That is the self you were before something happened which caused you to *believe* you are a sinner. The *belief that you are a sinner* is what allegedly created your "false self." One of the core doctrines of the Enneagram comes through the reintroduction of the late, fourth-century heresy known as Pelagianism.

> Pelagianism views humanity as basically good and morally unaffected by the Fall. It denies the imputation of Adam's sin, original sin, total depravity, and substitutionary atonement. It simultaneously views man as fundamentally good and in possession of libertarian free will. With regards to salvation, it teaches that man has the ability in and of himself (apart from divine aid) to obey God and earn eternal salvation. Pelagianism is overwhelmingly incompatible with the Bible and was historically opposed by Augustine (354-430), Bishop of Hippo, leading to its condemnation as a heresy at Council of Carthage in 418 A.D.. These condemnations were summarily ratified at the Council of Ephesus (A.D. 431).[13]

As Allegra Hobbs recounts it in her online article "The Self-Help Movement That Is Upending American Christianity," Sarajane Case followed a similar path:

Sarajane Case remembers the precise moment she severed her lifelong relationship with Christianity. Her uneasiness had been building over time, sparked by the realization that her queer friends were not at home in the church she loved. But the end came suddenly and quietly: In 2010, at the end of a yoga class, the instructor told Case and the other attendees to thank themselves for showing up.

"That just broke something in me," she says.

What Case realized in that moment was that she had never truly thanked herself for anything. "Everything I had ever done in my life I was like, 'All credit to God, everything good is God, I am terrible, anything good in me is God.'"

Case had grown up going to church every Sunday, had attended a Southern Baptist university, and had effectively built her identity around her devoutness. That day in 2010, she realized that religion made her feel she had to downplay her own identity as a form of religious devotion. So she stopped.[14]

Case describes a religious background of faithful church attendance, but we do not know what sort of church it was or the depth of any teaching on the essentials. She attended Gardner-Webb University (which claims to be a "private, Christian, Baptist-related university" on their website); but again, what did the school teach, and how much did she understand of the essentials of the faith? Again, no information is given. It sounds as though she may have left the church in 2010 with only part of the story. From her statement regarding her homosexual friends feeling "not at home in the church," it's also evident she had already imbibed much from our "feelings-trump-everything" culture.

Alegra Hobbs also seems less than knowledgeable in these areas of theology. She attempts to ascribe Case's struggles—against the idea that we are sinners by nature and by choice—to Calvinism, when actually, this is one of the core teachings of Scripture!

Let's take a look at her objection to this doctrine, one step at a time. Her belief that "anything good in me is God" is completely true according to the Bible. How many people in history came into existence "good?" The answer, biblically at least, is three: Adam and Eve, who were created; and Christ Jesus, Who was fully God incarnate and was also fully human. God is, by nature, good. It is *inherent* in His being. When the Son took on human flesh, His human nature—like Adam and Eve's prior to the Fall—was "good." Where did the "good" nature—for Adam, Eve and the humanity of Jesus Christ—originate? God!

Scripture teaches that Adam and Eve sinned—disobeyed God— and, thus, their nature was corrupted. With the exception of Jesus Christ, the sin nature has passed down to all of their descendants, including us (cf. Genesis 5:3); and we now are "*by nature children of wrath, like the rest of mankind*" (Ephesians 2:3). In Romans 7:18, the Apostle Paul speaks to this issue as he is grappling with the question of why he does the wrong that he does, especially since *he wants to do good;* and he writes, "*For I know that nothing good dwells in me, that is, in my flesh.*" It isn't simply that we are sinners by nature; that there is nothing inherently good in us; that there is no "good self" longing to be set free. We are also sinners by our own volition. Sin is something we *do*. We are incapable *in ourselves* of doing even the good we want to do! As Paul writes, "*for all have sinned and fall short of the glory of God*" (Romans 3:23).

But here is the very important piece of information which Enneagram celebrities, "master teachers," and teachers miss: *God does not leave those who are born again in that sorry state.* (Romans 10:9-13, 1 Corinthians 15:1-4 *and other passages explain the Gospel of salvation is belief in the death, burial, and physical resurrection of Jesus and calling on Him as God to be saved or born-again.*) The Apostle said there was "*nothing good*" in his "*flesh*"—his old nature—and he describes our natural condition as being sinners separated from God. Fortunately, he doesn't stop there. He goes on to teach that we become "*a new creation*" "*in Christ.*" As a new creature in Christ,

> *I have the desire to do what is right, but not the ability* [in his old nature] *to carry it out. For I do not do the good I want, but the evil I do not want is what I keep on doing. Now, if I do what I do not want* [sin]*, it is no longer I who do it, but sin* [his old nature] *that dwells within me.*" (Romans 7:18b-20)

> *Therefore, if anyone is in Christ, he is a new creation.*

The old has passed away; behold, the new has come. (2 Corinthians 5:17)

Thus, we *now* have *"peace with God"* (Romans 5:1), we *"put on Christ"* (Galatians 3:27); and as a new creation, we have "good" which God gives us. God immediately looks upon us as completely new creatures—*clothed in the righteousness of His son!* He views Christians with love, not disdain.

Case, Hobbs, and the Enneagram teachers either do not know or fail to understand the distinction between human *value* and human *goodness* when compared to the standard of God's goodness and holiness. The fact that all true goodness comes from God does not mean that even sinful human beings are worthless in God's eyes. He considered human beings so valuable, loved us so much, that He sent His only Son Jesus Christ to die for us so we could be saved and ultimately completely perfected (cf. John 3:16-18). As we stand now in Christ, we have two natures—the new creature in Christ and the sinful old nature—engaged in all-out war within us (Romans 7:15-23). There is no doubt; it is often distressing and certainly disconcerting to live with the two natures fighting within us. Who will deliver us from this painful predicament, *"this body of death"* as Paul refers to it in Romans 7:24? *"Thanks be to God,"* Paul writes, *"who gives us the victory through our Lord Jesus Christ"* (1 Corinthians 15:57).

Complete deliverance from the sin nature is not something we experience in this life. We do have to fight it all the while we are here on earth in our mortal bodies. But our redemption is coming … it is sure. So, our deliverance involves *waiting on the Lord*. People either do not know that, or they simply refuse to bear up under the admittedly unpleasant dual-nature dilemma while they wait. Is God evil in making us wait and suffer the battle within? No, He holds back from destroying evil for the *good of others*, so that all have a chance to turn to Him for salvation! As Jesus said, rooting out the tares (weeds) before the time will hurt the wheat (Matthew 13:29-30). Christians having to live for a time with the two natures is just a facet of the so-called "problem of evil." God allows evil for a time until, metaphorically, all the wheat has been brought safely into the barn.

Another thing often missed in self-centered "spiritual paths" like the Enneagram, as noted in the film *American Gospel: Christ Alone*, is that we are not the central character in Scripture with God as a supporting actor. *God* is the central character. It is the story of *God's creation, His love* for us, *His provision for our redemption* to give us peace with Him eternally, and, finally, *His total eradication of evil*. It appears this God-centered essential truth is lost on Enneagram proponents.

"This is a Football"

In 1961, Vince Lombardi, who at that time was the coach of the Green Bay Packers, walked into the training camp locker room of 38 players. His opening welcome was a phrase which began a tradition he continued for the rest of his career. The background of his remarks was the sad fact that the Green Bay Packers had ended the previous season by losing to the Philadelphia Eagles in the NFL championship by squandering their lead late in the fourth quarter. As he entered the locker room, Vince Lombardi held up a football and stated, "Gentlemen, this is a football." That was, of course, a fairly rudimentary—some might say self-evident—remark. According to author David Maraniss, in his best-selling book *When Pride Still Mattered: A Life of Vince Lombardi*, Lombardi then went on to explain the basic game of football. From there, he took the team out onto the field and explained the parts of the field. In other words, he went back to basics.

In Hebrews 5:11-14, we have a sort of biblical equivalent of this as the author of Hebrews warns about the dangers of forgetting the basics:

> *About this we have much to say, and it is hard to explain, since you have become <u>dull of hearing.</u> For though by this time you ought to be teachers, you need someone to teach you again the basic principles of the oracles of God. You need milk, not solid food, for everyone who lives on milk is unskilled in the word of righteousness, since he is a child. But solid food is for the mature, for those who have their <u>powers of discernment trained by constant practice</u> to distinguish good from evil.* (Hebrews 5:11-14)

Notice two things here. First, the basics had to be retaught to those who had learned them but had not used them. Second, *"powers of discernment"* are *"trained by constant practice."* The old cliché "Use it or lose it" comes to mind. Please recall what we said earlier concerning the 2016 LifeWay Research survey:

- 71% of evangelicals "said that Jesus was the first being God created."
- 56% agreed that "the Holy Spirit is a divine force but not a personal being;" and if a personal being, not equal with the Father.
- 51% agreed that "God accepts the worship of all religions including Christianity, Judaism, and Islam."

There are many distractions and lots of varied, non-biblical opinions and alleged "truths" being *shouted* at us and our children from the culture through movies, TV, popular music; and this is even taught to children in school. New Age, mystical "tools" such as the Enneagram are being offered even in some churches. And yet, at this critical juncture—with the historic Christian faith under attack from all sides—too many Christians, though still sitting in church, have grown *"dull of hearing"* (Hebrews 5:11), not toward the culture, but to the truth. It may just be a good first step to hold up the Bible when preaching and open with, "This is Christianity." Then should follow a careful and systematic teaching on the essentials of the faith with emphasis on the extreme importance of knowing and keeping one's heart and mind on what is true, and how to distinguish between truth and error in the spiritual area.

We think it quite possible that many Christians don't really appreciate the danger of wandering around looking for "truth" in all the wrong places. People, including Christians, are often on a quest for something new—perhaps something "deep" and rather mysterious. Mystical, New Age beliefs are *not* new, they are as old as ancient paganism; but they come across as "deep and mysterious," certainly. Many, if not most, Evangelicals have rejected New Age mysticism as heresy for a good many years now; but perhaps the children didn't get the memo. The young probably do not recognize these teachings for what they are, and they may never have been familiar with those old lies to begin with. "No, this is something new!" "I can feel better about myself!" "I can fix myself!" "I can, perhaps, fix my friends; who really could use some fixing as well!" They, as well as any older Christians, need to learn about wolves in sheeps' clothing who are seeking to turn them away from their faith. So, we see it is not for their own welfare alone that people need to truly *know* and understand their faith. Their welfare—if not, indeed, the eternal destinies—of their children, grandchildren and other loved ones, may very well depend upon their knowing and being able to articulate these truths. Babes in the faith cannot even help themselves, let alone help anyone else. This isn't new territory or some new revolutionary concept. YHWH (a.k.a. the LORD) told the nation of Israel:

> *Hear, O Israel: The LORD our God, the LORD is one. You shall love the LORD your God with all your heart and with all your soul and with all your might. And these words that I command you today shall be on your heart. You shall teach them diligently to your children, and shall talk of them when you sit in your house, and when you walk by the way, and when you lie down, and when you rise. You shall bind them as a sign on your hand, and they shall be as frontlets between your eyes. You shall write them on the doorposts of your house and on your gates.* (Deuteronomy 6:4-9)

How were they to love God? By ...

- Having His words in their hearts.
- Teaching them diligently to their children.
- Talking and thinking about His Word when they are sitting at home, walking somewhere, being the last thing before they go to sleep, and the first thing when they get up.
- Having it on display and readily accessible *everywhere*!

As the Word of God becomes central to the evaluation of everything we do or is going on around us, it becomes the standard by which any and all new teaching is tested.

This is Christianity

We know *many* pastors who are Christ-centered, biblically informed, and hold to Sola Scriptura ("Scripture alone") for faith and practice. We hold these godly men in high esteem and thank God for them. Pastors and elders are charged with the task of safeguarding the flock from predators, false teachers, and false teachings which would invade from the outside or rise up from within:

> *Pay careful attention to yourselves and to all the flock, in which the Holy Spirit has made you overseers, to care for the church of God, which he obtained with his own blood. I know that after my departure fierce wolves will come in among you, not sparing the flock; and from among your own selves will arise men speaking twisted things, to draw away the disciples after them. Therefore, be alert, remembering that for three years I did not cease night or day to admonish every one with tears.* (Acts 20:28-31)

When the Apostle Paul wrote his first letter to Timothy (whom he had left in Ephesus), he structured it with a flow derived from this charge to the elders in Acts. In 1 Timothy 1:1-11, Paul instructs Timothy to take a public stand, before the congregation against false teaching:

> *As I urged you when I was going to Macedonia, remain at Ephesus so that you may charge certain persons not to teach any different doctrine* (1 Timothy 1:3)

In 1 Timothy 3, Paul lays out the qualifications for leadership beginning in 1 Timothy 3:1:

> *The saying is trustworthy: If anyone aspires to the office of overseer, he desires a noble task.* (1 Timothy 3:1)

The word *episkopes* (English transliteration of original Greek word) is translated here as *bishop* or *overseer.* It describes the work which is being carried out in Acts 20:17-21, where the Greek word *presbuteros* is used and translated *elder* for the same position. Paul's main considerations are a leader's spiritual life and biblical understanding first and foremost. According to 1 Timothy 4:1-5, these qualifications are necessary so that the elders, charged with guarding the flock, are *capable* of recognizing false teachers, false teachings, and taking steps necessary to protect the flock:

> *Now the Spirit expressly says that in later times some will depart from the faith by devoting themselves to deceitful spirits and teachings of demons* (1 Timothy 4:1)

How was this prophesied apostasy of the latter times to be addressed? The leadership was to preach and teach the Word diligently, to urge the flock to be alert to strange teachings, and to remain true to the faith:

> *devote yourself to the public reading of Scripture, to exhortation, to teaching.* (1 Timothy 4:13)

About three or four years later Paul followed up with his second Letter to Timothy, which follows a similar theme. In the second chapter he writes,

> *And the things which you have heard from me in the presence of many witnesses, these entrust to faithful men, who will <u>be able to teach others also.</u>* (2 Timothy 2:2)

In order to "*be able to teach others also,*" they would need to know and understand the essentials and be able to identify false teachings. He then goes on to talk about the attitudes and abilities of a "*servant*":

> *And <u>the Lord's servant must not be quarrelsome but kind to everyone</u>, able to teach, patiently enduring evil, <u>correcting his opponents with gentleness</u>. God may perhaps grant them repentance leading to a knowledge of the truth, and they may come to their senses and escape from the snare of the devil, after being captured by him to do his will.* (2 Timothy 2:24-26)

Not only were the elders to be equipped to protect the flock from receiving false teachers, but they were to lovingly attempt a gentle rescue of those who had embraced and been blinded by false teaching. In 2 Timothy 3, Paul describes the future apostasy in more detail (2 Timothy 3:1-9), and he returns to emphasizing the importance of God's Word:

> *All Scripture is breathed out by God and profitable for teaching, for reproof, for correction, and for training in righteousness, that the man of God may be complete, equipped for every good work.* (2 Timothy 3:16-17)

Paul begins the very next chapter:

> *I charge you in the presence of God and of Christ Jesus, who is to judge the living and the dead, and by his appearing and his kingdom: preach the word; be ready in season and out of season; reprove, rebuke, and exhort, with complete patience and teaching.* (2 Timothy 4:1-2)

Although the elders were to be as gentle and kind as possible in dealing with false teachers, they were *publicly* to correct and rebuke them—again for the purpose of protecting the flock. Just to make sure Timothy and the leaders he is training understand the *absolute necessity* of correcting false teaching, Paul also warns them that false teaching will decimate the church in later times:

> *For the time is coming when people will not endure sound teaching, but having itching ears they will accumulate for themselves teachers to suit their own passions, and will turn away from listening to the truth and wander off into myths.* (2 Timothy 4:3-4)

In between Paul's first and second letter to Timothy, he wrote to the same church (in Ephesus) in probably 61 or 62 A.D., and he includes this:

> *And he gave them apostles, the prophets, the evangelists, the shepherds and teachers, to equip the saints for the work*

of ministry, for building up the body of Christ, until we all attain to the unity of the faith and of the knowledge of the Son of God, to mature manhood, to the measure of the stature of the fullness of Christ, so that we may no longer be children, tossed to and fro by the waves and carried about by every wind of doctrine, by human cunning, by craftiness in deceitful schemes. (Ephesians 4:11-13)

The saints (believers) are to be trained and enabled to do "*the work of ministry.*" Rather than turning away from the faith and flocking to false teachers, as will occur in later times, Paul wanted *all believers*—not just elders and pastors—to grow up to "*mature manhood*" in the faith "*so that we may no longer be children, tossed to and fro by the waves and carried about by every wind of doctrine, by human cunning, by craftiness in deceitful schemes.*" False teachers are *cunning, crafty,* and *deceitful schemers.* Pastors and teachers are to protect the flock *and to teach them how to protect themselves and others!*

As pastors and leaders are training and equipping believers how to read, understand, and apply the Word of God, they grow spiritually, and the church grows spiritually. In the process, all believers will be equipped to carry out the mission of the church and develop their own spiritual gifts to proclaim the Gospel to the world of unbelievers. No believer is excused from the serious work of discerning truth from error. The Gospel cannot be proclaimed if the Gospel is not fully understood by those who would share it.

In today's culture, it is extremely difficult to keep up with all of the trends, spiritual celebrities, and false teachers who rise up, gain a following, and begin enticing those in the churches. Apologetics, discernment ministries, and missionaries to cults and non-Christian religions have a narrow focus and serve pastors and the body of Christ. It is an encouragement, in an age when the culture in the United States has become increasingly pagan, to see there is also a growth in the area of well-trained apologists. They are a resource which can be helpful in your church.

Won't Unbelievers be Offended?

With all of the teaching in Scripture warning against heresy and false teachers, it is obvious that discernment and sound, scriptural teaching is of utmost importance to the health of the church in any era but, perhaps, most especially now. Yet, many worry that teaching Scripture might cause offense to unbelievers. A word of warning here: Some may not like our response. The church isn't primarily for unbelievers. It is primarily for believers. *All* the New Testament letters are written to the pastors, elders, and believers in first-century churches, where all we have outlined was to be carried out publicly and privately. There are not many warnings in Scripture concerning protecting unbelievers from being offended by Scripture or sound doctrinal teaching. In fact, there are none. There *are* warnings about giving *unnecessary offense* by dealing with people in a harsh manner and with a lack of respect. It seems Paul did not expect the church to be full of unbelievers. As he is addressing bad behavior in the Corinthian church, he speaks about the issue of the sign gifts and prophecy, where he writes:

> *If, therefore, the whole church comes together and all speak in tongues, and outsiders or unbelievers enter* (1 Corinthians 14:23)

> *But if all prophesy, and an unbeliever or outsider enters* (1 Corinthians 14:24)

If *"outsiders or unbelievers enter"* seems to imply that most people in a given church would be believers. Church is where the ministry of the church takes place *for the family of God*. It is for believers.

Where is the Apostle Paul's strategy for enticing unbelievers into the church in order to sneak up on them with the Gospel? It isn't there. Proclamation of the Gospel to unbelievers is the *mission* of the church, something for which *all believers* are to be trained and discipled! The *ministry* of the church is what happens when believers gather, whereas the *mission* of the church is what they are to do when they leave and rejoin the world of unbelievers. Should unbelievers feel welcomed in the church? ABSOLUTELY! That is the very reason Paul was concerned about the chaos and pandemonium which was happening in the Corinthian church. Unbelievers should be welcomed and challenged by what is taught and not terrified by frenzy and bedlam.

Think of it this way: At a family gathering for Thanksgiving or Christmas, the family will have certain traditions, ways of expressing love and care for one another. Suppose a family member brings a friend to dinner. The family does not throw their traditions out the window, but instead invites them in to join in with what the family is already doing. When believers gather, that is family time. There are particular things to be done at the "Christian family" gathering. There is the worship and adoration of the one, true God. There is praying with and for one another as family. There is the reading and teaching of the Word of God. And there is the presentation and reminders of certain, very important teachings—the basics:

- There is one, true God; and in the nature of that One true God is three co-equal, co-eternal Persons.
- God is omniscient (knows everything), omnipotent (is all powerful), and omnipresent (is present everywhere).
- God created everything which came into being.
- Humans are fallen and separated from God due to sin.
- God the Son took on human nature, lived a perfect life which we are unable to live, sacrificed His incarnated life in a horrible death we deserve, and physically raised Himself from the dead to secure salvation for those who believe.
- God communicates to us through His inspired, inerrant Scripture.
- The Word of God, taught by the people of God with the power of the Holy Spirit, also equips and matures God's people to be missionaries to an unbelieving world.

A "Golden Calf" has been brought into the sanctuaries of many churches. While not intended by the pastors and elders to replace God, it serves as an alternative way to *feel more spiritual,* for it seems God Himself is simply not enough. Richard Rohr and the secret of the Enneagram is only the most recent syncretistic inclusion of pagan ritual and worship with the Word of God. Biblically faithful churches need to take a stand against it and to heed these words written by the Apostle Paul to a young pastor long ago:

> *charge certain persons not to teach any different doctrine,*
> *nor to devote themselves to myths and endless genealogies,*
> *which promote speculations rather than the stewardship from*
> *God that is by faith.* (1 Timothy 1:3-4)

CHAPTER 8

One Last Question: Can God Redeem Anything?

As we have researched, written, and answered questions about this newest fad sweeping through the church, a recurring question surfaces from those who currently are using the Enneagram. They ask: "Can't God redeem anything?"

In those discussions, we take time to expose the various claims of the Enneagram as being ancient are false; and we reveal it was originally invented by a Russian mystic (George I. Gurdjieff) as the cosmic explanation for everything. We track the changes and additions made by New Agers Oscar Ichazo and Claudio Naranjo, who have twisted and distorted the original meaning of the Enneagram through the direction of spirit beings and automatic writing. Finally, we show how Richard Rohr incorporates his theology of panentheism and perennialism—heretical worldviews unto themselves—into the occult system of the Enneagram. He also teaches each Enneagram number is an individual path back to the realization we have never sinned. In his view, we have *always* been sinless; and we *are ourselves "The Christ,"* since "The Christ" is the cosmos of which we are a part (see chapter 6).

The concept of being able to somehow "Christianize" the Enneagram is a fairly new development. This new idea of a separate

"Christianized Enneagram" probably got its start with the arrival on the scene of Christian Enneagram coaches like Beth McCord and her husband Jeff, who is a pastor. On their website, they write:

> Beth is now leading the industry in simplifying the deep truths of the Enneagram from a Biblical perspective.[1]

This could at least imply they have stripped the Enneagram of its occultism, false historical claims, and false teaching; and what is left is a new, biblical Enneagram. But is that true? In Beth's biographical material, she claims she has been teaching the Enneagram for between 17-20 years. She also claims she has:

> been trained by the best Enneagram experts and pouring hundreds of hours into advanced certifications, Beth is now leading the industry in simplifying the deep truths of the Enneagram from a Biblical perspective.[2]

Here we encounter the first problem in her claims. Without exception, "the best Enneagram experts" who are Beth McCord's teachers—Helen Palmer, Russ Hudson, David Daniels, Jessica Dibbs and Kathrine Fauvre—are all New Agers. So, when we learn about the McCords' leadership of marriage and relationship workshops in venues far and wide, we rightly should be quite concerned. On the Misty Phillip's (1971-) *By His Grace* podcast "Episode 49: Marriage and the Enneagram: Beth and Jeff McCord,"[3] time is spent suggesting God can use or redeem anything. But is that, itself, a biblical claim? What biblical principles should guide us here?

It seems unwise to make a blanket statement like "God can use anything." For one thing, even though God can use what the Devil does to accomplish His will, that does not mean we should invite the Devil into the church pulpit. Often this claim or a similar one—"God can redeem anything"—is used to defend questionable practices.

First Principle: God's Character

First, God does not go against his character. For example, God cannot lie. God is just, and His nature is truth and goodness; so he cannot lie, do evil, or tolerate sin. This is all clearly taught in

Scripture. Would one who argues that God can redeem anything propose we are free to employ any of the following for Christian growth and guidance?

> The Ouija Board
> Astrology
> Tarot Cards
> Palmistry
> Phrenology
> Energy healing like Reiki
> Casting spells

Would God use a so-called "Christianized version" of any of these? If the answer is "no," then we realize there are limitations on the idea of "redeeming anything." We may use anything which God approves; but we may not use anything which God forbids. This is not only biblical, it is also good, common sense!

Second Principle: God's Use Does Not Mean God's Approval.

In the Bible, God uses bad people and bad situations, but He does so without endorsing their character or bad actions. For example: God used Balaam, a diviner and false prophet, to bless Israel (see account starting in Numbers 22). Balaam was trying to curse Israel for financial gain, but instead, God used Balaam to bless His people Israel.

Scripture goes on to give the details that God's use of Balaam does not indicate God was okay with Balaam's profession (diviner and false prophet) or actions. In fact, the New Testament gives us three condemnations of Balaam:

> *Forsaking the right way, they have gone astray. They have followed the way of Balaam, the son of Beor, who loved gain from wrongdoing,* (2 Peter 2:15)

> *Woe to them! For they walked in the way of Cain and abandoned themselves for the sake of gain to Balaam's error and perished in Korah's rebellion.* (Jude 1:11)

> *But I have a few things against you: you have some there*
> *who hold the teaching of Balaam, who taught Balak to put a*
> *stumbling block before the sons of Israel, so that they might*
> *eat food sacrificed to idols and practice sexual immorality.*
> (Revelation 2:14)

Someone might ask, "What about the Magi, the astrologers from the east, who followed a remarkable star?" Their inclusion in the historic narrative in Matthew 2, and the fact that God directed them to depart another way to keep Herod in the dark, does not in any way suggest an endorsement of astrology.

God used Joseph being sold into slavery to bring about his purposes for Egypt and his people (Genesis 50:20). Neither did God endorse the actions of Joseph's brothers, which Joseph pointed out were "evil." Nor did God endorse the brutal oppression of Israel by Egypt's rulers.

God used Assyria and Babylon to capture Israel and Judah as a form of discipline for His people; but God did not endorse the beliefs or cruelty of those kingdoms.

God used a *"thorn in the flesh, a messenger from Satan"* (2 Corinthians 12:7) to humble Paul, but God does not endorse this *"messenger"*—whatever it was. It was God's prerogative to do this, but Paul was not using anything from Satan.

There is a distinction between God's use of a person or situation, and *God's endorsement* or *approval* of evil.

Third Principle: There is a great distinction between what God does, and what we can do.

In all the aforementioned examples of God repurposing the actions He does not approve—an evil ruler, Balaam, or astrologers (such as the Magi), God is the one who decides whom, and what to use. Even if "God can use anything," that does not mean *we* can use anything.

Fourth Principle: God abhors certain practices connected to pagan worship and spiritual activity.

In Deuteronomy 18:10-14, God names and forbids several

practices that were done in conjunction with the worship of false gods.

It is evil and forbidden to contact the dead; therefore, using a Ouija Board or consulting a medium is wrong. (God also specifically condemns consulting mediums at Deuteronomy 18:11.) God brought back Samuel, who had died, to reprimand and pronounce judgement on King Saul; and God allowed three disciples to see Moses and Elijah with Jesus. But God did this by *His power*, at *His initiative*, and for *His own purposes*.

Neither of these situations involve a mere human contacting the dead,[4] nor do these events indicate that God has "redeemed" the practice of contacting the dead—an activity which God has forbidden. In fact, in 1 Chronicles 10:13-14, God states clearly that one reason Saul was killed was because he consulted a medium:

> *So, Saul died for his breach of faith. He broke faith with the LORD in that he did not keep the command of the LORD, and also consulted a medium, seeking guidance. He did not seek guidance from the LORD. Therefore, the LORD put him to death and turned the kingdom over to David the son of Jesse.* (1 Chronicles 10:13-14)

Is it okay to use divination—such as Tarot cards or astrology—as long as one is not worshiping a false god? No, God *does not* give that exception. Such practices are forbidden, period!

Will God redeem everything?

God's Word is quite clear that God *will redeem* those who have trusted in Christ; and He will redeem creation—make a *"new heaven"* and *"new earth"* (Revelation 21:1). However, He *will not redeem* other things, but rather cast them into the Lake of Fire: Satan, Satan's angels, death, and those who have rejected him (Revelation 19:20; Revelation 20:10, 14-15; 21:8).

Will witchcraft be redeemed? No.
Will sorcery be redeemed? No.
Will astrology be redeemed? No.
The list could go on. (See Revelation 21:8 and Revelation 22:15.)

The Enneagram

Even apart from biblical and doctrinal questions, at this point in time, the Enneagram has not been verified as a legitimate personality profiling tool. Back in 1992, when Mitch Pacwa was warning Roman Catholics of its dangers in his book *Catholics and the New Age: How Good People Are Being Drawn into Jungian Psychology, the Enneagram, and the Age of Aquarius*, he expressed concern over the lack of "objective scientific research into the enneagram."[5] After he points out the lack of any objective testing and reliance only on claims of occultists and anecdotal evidence, Pacwa goes on to make a very important point:

> In fact, because objective study of the enneagram does not exist, there are no norms for deciding who is an authentic or qualified enneagram teacher. No test, no standards, no board of examination exists, so most enneagram "experts" have that title through self-declaration and workshop advertising. People do not go to doctors and psychologists unless that practitioner is tested and licensed. Should not some similar requirement be made of enneagram teachers, who not only explain what your personality is like but make recommendation about what you should be like? Until such verification of the enneagram occurs, resulting in ways to discern who has enneagram expertise, I recommend that people not patronize the workshops, seminars, and retreats.[6]

To our knowledge only one credible test has been performed on the Enneagram since Pacwa raised this issue in 1992. Jay Medenwalt, an apologist working on his Ph.D. in social psychology, did a psychometric analysis and published his findings in January 2019.[7] He notes in the conclusion of his paper *"The Enneagram, Science, and Christianity—Part 1"*[8]:

> Any scientist who studies personality would simply look at the reliability scores and conclude the [Enneagram] test is not accurate enough to be helpful, and therefore, they wouldn't use it because the potential for harm will be too high.

The Enneagram has no worth even in the field of psychology! It is, therefore, useless; and it offers nothing but deception.

Yet, even if it were somehow "useful" in psychology, that would hardly sanction its use by Christians. There are many "useful" things that are forbidden to a believer. Stealing may seem "useful" to a person who values possessions over morality. Murder could even be considered "useful" in some contexts as long as right and wrong were not taken into the equation. The Enneagram is a direct product of gnostic, occult, and New Age beliefs going back to Gurdjieff, and then it was advanced through Oscar Ichazo and Claudio Naranjo—all of whom regularly engaged in practices forbidden by God. Therefore, the Enneagram has no redemption from a biblical perspective.

From there, New Age therapists and counselors added their own layers of New Age spirituality to it; so that it became a satisfyingly complex tool for those with a New Age worldview. The New Age does not care about objective standards and does not even accept the idea of objective truth. So, an invalid tool like the Enneagram is ideal in the New Age, because it is flexible and malleable. As we have pointed out, many Christian Enneagram teachers, like Beth McCord, were trained by New Age teachers; and any certifications one may claim were given by New Age Enneagram organizations.

The Enneagram is not spiritually neutral.

Having myself (Marcia) been involved in the occult practices of astrology, contacting the dead, using divinatory tools (Numerology, astrology, Tarot), and having spirit guides, I can say with 100% confidence that nothing that is a product of these practices or of New Age beliefs is beneficial for anyone; and it is always spiritually harmful *at the least.*

Can one make the Enneagram Christian?

Some have argued that one can remove the New Age worldviews and insert Christian ones. But how does that work with a tool that is fraudulent, invalid, and occultic in the first place? The perfect analogy is astrology. One could redefine the Zodiac signs and planets with certain positive, biblical traits (like the fruit of the Spirit or the

12 tribes of Israel), but how would that make Astrology valid? The use of a tool with no spiritual or psychological validity—which was fabricated in the occult, for occult purposes, and advanced by New Agers—cannot impart truth, useful information about you, God, or help anyone grow closer to God.

The Final Twist

The final twist on the Enneagram, to make it even more deceptive (at least to Christians), was to put it into the hands of someone who is "Christian" in name only, but who likely would be *perceived* as Christian: Richard Rohr. We contend Rohr departs from *"the faith that was once for all delivered to the saints"* (Jude 1:3) in almost all the essentials of the historic Christian faith: Man's sin and need for redemption; God and creation; the nature of Jesus Christ; and the Atonement. Rohr's teachings on these are contrary to the historic, biblical, Christian faith and present a false Jesus, a false Christ, and a false Gospel.

Rohr is a huge reason why and how the Enneagram came into the church—first in the progressive church and then in the church at large. Since then, it has gained rapid momentum due to books published, classes, seminars, and retreats taught by Rohr's students and disciples. (He mentored Christopher Heuertz, author of *The Sacred Enneagram,* and Suzanne Stabile, co-author of *The Road Back to You*).

If the Enneagram had stemmed from scientific, psychological studies, testing, and research and afterward had been used in the New Age, one could, perhaps, argue that Christians could still use it by going back to its original model. But there is no such model for the Enneagram. It originated with occult mystic George Gurdjieff, and it had no personality types. (Astrology also originally had nothing to do with personality.)[9] Perhaps a final word from the Scriptures is in order:

> *Do not turn to mediums or necromancers; do not seek them out, and so make yourselves unclean by them: I am the LORD your God.* (Leviticus 19:31)

ENDNOTES

Chapter 1— Enneagram 101: The Road Map

1 Jonathan Merritt. "What is the 'Enneagram,' and why are Christians suddenly so enamored by it," *Religious News Service* (September 5, 2017); https://religionnews.com/2017/09/05/what-is-the-enneagram-and-why-are-christians-suddenly-so-enamored-by-it/.

2 Ian Morgan Cron and Suzanne Stabile. *The Road Back to You: An Enneagram Journey to Self-Discovery* (Downers Grove, IL: InterVarsity Press, 2016).

3 Christopher L.Heuertz. *The Sacred Enneagram* (Grand Rapids, MI: Zondervan Publishing, 2017).

4 "Desert Fathers," *Wikipedia, The Free Encyclopedia*; https://en.wikipedia.org/wiki/Desert_Fathers.

5 This is an adaptation and expansion of Marcia Montenegro's "The Fictions and Facts of the Enneagram," *Christian Answers for the New Age*; http://christiananswersforthenewage.org/Articles_FictionFactsEnneagram.aspx.

6 For scholarly research concluding that the Enneagram originated with George Gurdjieff, see see James Moore who has a book that can be downloaded in PDF. Here is one of his articles: James Moore. "The Enneagram: A Developmental Study," *The RunningFather Blog;* https://runningfather.wordpress.com/2013/03/25/enneagram-a-developmental-study-james-moore/.

7 Jim Aldrich (aka Running Son). "Early Enneagram History: Naranjo, Ichazo, and the School, Part I," *The Running Father Blog*; https://runningfather.wordpress.com/2013/03/24/early-enneagram-history-naranjo-ichazo-and-the-school/.

8 Marcia Montenegro. "The Origins of the Enneagram—Marcia Montenegro," *YouTube* video. (Brandon Kimber, who did the film *The American Gospel: in Christ Alone,* filmed Marcia speaking on the Enneagram). The video clip of Naranjo's admission occurs at the 2:30-minute mark. (We also have Naranjo's interview on file.); https://www.youtube.com/watch?v=k9Jo90cl7Io.
9 Ibid., Naranjo's admission occurs at the 3:15-minute mark.
10 Richard Rohr. "The Enneagram as a tool for spiritual discernment." *YouTube* video. Beginning at the 4:00-minute mark. (We also have video on file.); https://www.youtube.com/watch?v=Aq9nRszFcM8
11 Richard Rohr. "Richard Rohr—Why Do We Misunderstand John 14:6?" *YouTube* video. In the short, 1:12-minute video, Richard Rohr asserts that Contemplation is to unlearn and "we have a lot of unlearning to do;" https://www.youtube.com/watch?v=03ID8ttKa7E.
12 Mitch Pacwa, SJ. "Tell Me Who I Am, O Enneagram," *CRI Journal* (Fall 1991), posted online June 9, 2009; https://www.equip.org/article/tell-me-who-i-am-o-enneagram/. (Accessed 2/11/2020).
13 Marcia Montenegro. "The Enneagram GPS: Gnostic Path to Self" *Christian Answers for the New Age (CANA)* (March 2011); http://christiananswersforthenewage.org/Articles_Enneagram.html.

Chapter 2— Forbidden Fruit

1 "comfortable in (one's) own skin," *The Free Dictionary;* https://idioms.thefreedictionary.com/comfortable+in+own+skin.
2 J.D. Barry, et. al.. "Genesis 3:1," *Faithlife Study Bible* (Bellingham, WA; Lexham Press: 2012, 2016).
3 A term and idea introduced by British psychoanalyst Donald Woods Winnicott in 1960. More will be said on "The True Self" further on.
4 *ra.ah* (הָאָר, 7200), *"to see, observe, perceive, get acquainted with, gain understanding, examine, look after (see to), choose, discover."* This verb occurs only in Moabite and all periods of Hebrew. It appears in the Bible about 1,300 times; W. E. Vine, et al., *Vine's Complete Expository Dictionary of Old and New Testament Words,* Vol. 1 (Nashville, TN: Thomas Nelson Publishers, 1996), p. 219.
5 Jeremy Myers does a very succinct job of the uses of the word *dead* in Scripture and demonstrates that in all cases it means separation from something. See "7 Uses of the word 'Dead' in the New Testament," *Redeeming God;* https://redeeminggod.com/dead-new-testament/.
6 T. Cabal, et al., *The Apologetics Study Bible: Real Questions, Straight Answers, Stronger Faith* (Nashville, TN: Holman Bible Publishers, 2007), p. 10.
7 *"The first, or earliest, declaration of the gospel (Gk. prōtos, 'first,' + euangelion, 'gospel') in Genesis 3:15, where God rebukes the serpent by*

predicting that Eve's offspring will crush the devil's offspring. Since the second century this verse has traditionally been seen as the first glimmer of the gospel that God's purpose in creation will be fulfilled in spite of the fall of humanity." In A.G. Patzia and A.J. Petrotta. *Pocket Dictionary of Biblical Studies* (Downers Grove, IL: InterVarsity Press, 2002), p. 96.

8 "Cosmos: A Personal Voyage," *Wikipedia, The Free Encyclopedia;* https://en.wikipedia.org/wiki/Cosmos:_A_Personal_Voyage.

9 Christopher L. Heuertz. *The Sacred Enneagram* (Grand Rapids, MI: Zondervan, 2017).

10 Ian Morgan Cron and Suzanne Stabile. *The Road Back to You: An Enneagram Journey to Self-Discovery* (Downers Grove, IL: InterVarsity Press, 2016).

11 "The Enneagram (Part 1)," Monday, May 26, 2014, *Richard Rohr's Daily Meditation;* (Copy on file.); https://myemail.constantcontact.com/Richard-Rohr-s-Meditation--The-Purpose-of-the-Enneagram.html?soid=1103098668616&aid=r3z0f6qxjmc.

12 Christian Answers for the New Age. Russ Hudson, New Ager, and co-Founder of the Enneagram Institute. *Facebook,* November 22, 2019; https://www.facebook.com/FormerNewAger/posts/10156333978412237.

13 Jonathan Merritt. "What is the 'Enneagram,' and why are Christians suddenly so enamored by it," *Religious News Service* (September 5, 2017); https://religionnews.com/2017/09/05/what-is-the-enneagram-and-why-are-christians-suddenly-so-enamored-by-it/.

14 Op. cit. "The Enneagram (Part 1)."

15 Op. cit. Jonathan Merritt.

16 Ian Morgan Cron and Suzanne Stabile. *The Road Back to You: An Enneagram Journey to Self-Discovery* (Downers Grove, IL: InterVarsity Press, 2016), p. 12.

17 Ibid., p. 15.

18 Ibid.

19 John Calvin. "The Institutes of the Christian Religion" *Christian Classics Ethereal Library* (Grand Rapids, MI), p.37; https://ccel.org/ccel/calvin/institutes/institutes/Page_37.html.

20 Ibid., p. 38; https://ccel.org/ccel/calvin/institutes/institutes/Page_38.html.

21 Ibid.

22 Ibid., p. 39; https://ccel.org/ccel/calvin/institutes/institutes/Page_39.html.

Chapter 3— Myth Taken

1 R.W. Yarbrough, D. A. Carson, Eds., *The Letters to Timothy and Titus* (Grand Rapids, MI; London: William B. Eerdmans Publishing Company, , 2018), p. 101.

2 W. E. Vine, et al., *Vine's Complete Expository Dictionary of Old and New Testament Words,* Vol. 2 (Nashville, TN; Thomas Nelson Publishers: 1996), p. 220.

3 *"At the beginning of the patriarchal period, when God promised a specific amount of territory to Abraham and his descendants, the importance of maintaining personal genealogies became more obvious. When the Israelite tribes came into existence after Jacob, the recording of family and community relationships assumed a new importance in the light of the necessity for establishing and maintaining the allotment of the land by tribal divisions. Once sedentary occupation of Palestine had taken place under Joshua and the land had been apportioned to the various tribes, the genealogical records were adduced as evidence of a legitimate title or claim to the property of one's ancestors."* R.K. Harrison, G.W. Bromiley, Ed. "Genealogy" *The International Standard Bible Encyclopedia,* Vol. 2 (Grand Rapids, MI: Wm. B. Eerdmans Publishing Company, Revised 1999), p. 425.

4 Ibid.

5 Christopher L.Heuertz. *The Sacred Enneagram* (Grand Rapids, MI: Zondervan Publishing, 2017), pg. 43. Kindle Edition.

6 Ibid.

7 "Pythagoras" (under Biographical Resources);" *Wikipedia, The Free Encyclopedia*; https://en.wikipedia.org/wiki/Pythagoras.

8 Op. cit. Christopher Heuertz, pp. 43-44.

9 Marcia Montenegro. "Kabbalah: Getting Back to the Garden" *CRI Journal* (June 11, 2009); https://www.equip.org/article/kabbalah-getting-back-to-the-garden/.

10 Op. cit. Christopher L. Heuertz, p. 44.

11 "Evagrius Ponticus: Christian Mystic," *Encyclopedia Britannica*; https://www.britannica.com/biography/Evagrius-Ponticus.

12 Personal correspondence on file.

13 Richard Rohr and Andreas Ebert (trans. Peter Heinegg). *Discovering the Enneagram: An Ancient Tool for a New Spiritual Journey* (New York, NY: Crossroad Publishing, 1992), p. xii and p. xv, emphasis added.

14 "Ramón Llull," *Wikipedia, The Free Encyclopedia;* https://en.wikipedia.org/wiki/Ramon_Llull.

15 "Richard Rohr says about Helen Palmer" *Enneagram.com* website; www.enneagram.com/helen_palmer.html. Helen Palmer is a psychic who has adopted the interchangeable term "intuitive."

16 Op. cit. Christopher L.Heuertz, p. 44.

17 Ibid.

18 Ian Mogan Cron homepage, https://ianmorgancron.com (Accessed 02/17/2020).

19 Ian Morgan Cron and Suzanne Stabile. *The Road Back to You: An*

Enneagram Journey to Self-Discovery (Downers Grove, IL: InterVarsity Press, 2016), p. 11, emphasis ours.
20 James Moore. "The Enneagram: A Developmental Study," *The RunningFather Blog;* https://runningfather.wordpress.com/2013/03/25/enneagram-a-developmental-study-james-moore/

Chapter 4 — Genesis of the Enneagram: From Gurdjieff to Rohr
1 N.P. Feldmeth. "Gnosticism," *Pocket Dictionary of Church History: Over 300 Terms Clearly and Concisely Defined* (Downers Grove, IL: InterVarsity Press, Academic, 2008), p. 53. (Asterisk in quote.)
2 A.M. Renwick, G. W. Bromiley Eds. "Gnosticism." *The International Standard Bible Encyclopedia* Vol. 2 (Grand Rapids, MI: Wm. B. Eerdmans Publishing, Revised), p. 489.
3 The Rev. Alexander Roberts, D.D. and James Donaldson, LL.D. (Eds), *The Ante-Nicene Fathers: Translations of the Writings of the Fathers Down to A.D. 325,* Vol. 1 (T & T Clark, Edinburgh; Grand Rapids, MI: Wm. B. Eerdmans Publishing, Reprinted 1989), p. 329.
4 Christopher L.Heuertz. *The Sacred Enneagram* (Grand Rapids, MI: Zondervan Publishing, 2017), pg. 44. Kindle Edition.
5 "P.D. Ouspensky," *Wikipedia, The Free Encyclopedia;* https://en.wikipedia.org/wiki/P._D._Ouspensky.
6 P.D. Ouspensky, *In Search of the Miraculous* (New York: Routledge, and Kegan Paul, 1950), p. 294; as quoted in "A Brief Report on the Origins of the Enneagram," *National Catholic Reporter (NCR)*; https://natcath.org/NCR_Online/documents/ennea2.htm.
7 For example, "Gurdjieff Sacred Dance—Movement 11," *YouTube* video; https://www.youtube.com/watch?v=VhM8PsEYX0M.
8 James Moore. "The Enneagram: A Developmental Study," *The RunningFather Blog;* https://runningfather.wordpress.com/2013/03/25/enneagram-a-developmental-study-james-moore/.
9 *"The whirling dance or Sufi whirling that is proverbially associated with dervishes is best known in the West by the practices (performances) of the Mevlevi order in Turkey, and is part of a formal ceremony known as the Sama. It is, however, also practiced by other orders."* From "Dervish," *Wikipedia, The Free Encyclopedia*; https://en.wikipedia.org/wiki/Dervish.
10 Bob Larson. *Larson's Book of World Religions and Alternative Spirituality* (Wheaton, IL: Tyndale House Publishers, 1982, 1989, 2004), p. 221.
11 Ibid., pp. 221-222. For more information on the dances and the "Law of Three" and the "Law of Seven," see the Gurdjieff-devoted website, *Awakening and Transformation;* https://awakeningandtransformation.com/gurdjieff-about-the-work.

12 P.D. Ouspensky, *In Search of the Miraculous* (New York: Routledge, and Kegan Paul, 1950), p. 44 as quoted by Brandon Medina in "The Enneagram: A History (Part 2)" *Theology Thinktank* blog, June 13, 2019 at https://theologythinktank.com/the-enneagram-a-history-part-2/.
13 Rodney Collin. "The Christian Mystery," *Holybooks.com* website (pdf online); https://www.holybooks.com/the-christian-mystery-by-rodney-collin/.
14 Rodney Collin. "Gurdjieff Becoming Conscious," *Consciousevolution.tv* website; https://www.consciousevolution.tv/conscious-evolution/rodney-collin-gurdjieff-becoming-conscious.php.
15 Ronald V. Huggins, Th.D. (Note on file.)
16 "Oscar Ichazo," *Wikipedia, The Free Encyclopedia*; https://en.wikipedia.org/wiki/Óscar_Ichazo.
17 *"According to the affidavit of Arica's Executive Director Elliot Dunderdale: The Arica system constitutes a body of practical and theoretical knowledge in the form of a nine-level hierarchy of training programs aimed at the total development of the human being. ... The Arica system observes that the human body and psyche is composed of nine independent yet interconnected systems. Particular imbalances within these systems are called 'fixations'. ... These nine separate components are represented by enneagons—nine pointed figures that map the human psyche. Ichazo writes that there are seven fundamental enneagons associated with the nine ego fixations. Thus, the enneagons constitute the structural maps of a human psyche ... [and] provide a guide through which a person may better understand oneself and one's interactions with others. ... An ego fixation is an accumulation of life experience organized during one's childhood and which shapes one's personality. Arica training seeks to overcome the control and influence of the ego fixations so that the individual may return to the inner balance with which he or she was born.*

"Ichazo's 'enneagons,' central to this lawsuit, are nine-pointed figures, enclosed in a circle, with straight lines connecting each point to two others. Each point corresponds to a given 'ego fixation' as represented in the following enneagon of the fixations."
Quoted from Florida Law Firm, ARICA INSTITUTE, INC., Plaintiff-Appellant, v.Helen PALMER and Harper & Row Publishers, Incorporated, Defendants-Appellees. No. 771, Docket 91-7859. United States Court of Appeals, Second Circuit. Argued Jan. 30, 1992. Decided July 22, 1992. http://floridalawfirm.com/arica.html.
18 Ibid.
19 "The Traditional Enneagram Overview," *The Enneagram Institute* website; https://www.enneagraminstitute.com/the-traditional-enneagram.

20 *"John Lilly who described his Arica studies in [i:9334d66c94] 'The
Eye of the Cyclone' [/i:9334d66c94] said that most of the material
he learned in Arica was facilitated by use of psychedelic drugs. The
problem was that insights gained during these drug trips could not be
easily transferred to daily life. Lilly parted company with Ichazo when he
sensed that if he continued as Ichazo's disciple, he would have to give up
his commitment to scientific and critical thinking.*

*"Ichazo's story kept changing. He claimed to be a Sufi, but never
substantiated his sources."*
Quoted from "Problems with Arica Institute," *Cult Education Institute*
website; https://forum.culteducation.com/read.php?12,4099.

21 For sources on Ichazo and Metatron, see John C. Lilly and Joseph
E. Hart, Charles T. Tart, Ed.. "The Arica Training," *Transpersonal
Psychologies* (New York, NY: Harper & Row, 1975), p. 342. From
footnote 16 in Dorothy Garrity Ranaghan, *A Closer Look at the
Enneagram* (South Bend, IN: Greenlawn Press, 1975), p. 9. For
more on Gurdjieff and Ichazo, see James Moore. "The Enneagram: A
Developmental Study," *The RunningFather Blog;* https://runningfather.
wordpress.com/2013/03/25/enneagram-a-developmental-study-james-
moore/.

22 "The origin of the Enneagram—Claudio Naranjo speaks - June 2010,"
YouTube video; starting at 1:45-minute mark. (Video on file.); http://bit.
ly/2lGphUr.

23 Ibid.

24 Nudity continues there today. "Must I Get Naked? Is Esalen a Nudist
Colony?" *Esalen* website; https://www.esalen.org/content/must-i-get-
naked-esalen-nudist-colony.

LSD was integral to the various "Human Potential" experiments.
Jan Irvin, "How Darwin, Huxley, and the Esalen Institute launched the
2012 and psychedelic revolutions—and began one of the largest mind
control operations in history." *LogosMedia* (August 28, 2012); https://
logosmedia.com/2012/08/how-darwin-huxley-and-the-esalen-institute-
launched-the-2012-and-psychedelic-revolutions-and-began-one-of-the-
largest-mind-control-operations-in-history/.

25 Dorothy Garrity Ranaghan, "A Closer Look at the Enneagram,"
(South Bend, IN: Greenlawn Press, 1975), p. 9.

26 Mitch Pacwa, SJ. *Catholics and the New Age: How Good People Are
Being Drawn into Jungian Psychology, the Enneagram, and the Age of
Aquarius* (Ann Arbor, MI: Servant Publications, 1992), pp. 108-109.

27 Ibid., pp. 111-112.

28 Mitch Pacwa, SJ. "Tell Me Who I Am, O Enneagram," *CRI Journal*
(Fall 1991), posted online June 9, 2009; https://www.equip.org/article/
tell-me-who-i-am-o-enneagram/. (Accessed 2/11/2020).

29 "How David Discovered the Enneagram," *DrDavidDaniels* website; http://drdaviddaniels.com/daviddaniels/discovering-the-enneagram/.

Chapter 5 — Richard Rohr: Which God Does He Serve?
1 J.J. Pilch. *Cultural Handbook to the Bible* (Grand Rapids, MI: William B. Eerdmans Publishing Company; Cambridge, U.K., 2012), p. 240.
2 See book review of Rohr's *The Universal Christ* by Marcia Montenegro. "'Who do men say that I am?' An Evaluation of Richard Rohr's *Universal Christ*" *Christian Answers for the New Age (CANA);* (First published April 2019.); http://www.christiananswersforthenewage. org/Articles_UniversalChrist.aspx.
3 Richard Rohr hasn't provided an actual definition of what "nondual" or "nonduality" means for him. But we understand from the examples he gives, there is no saved/unsaved dichotomy, different classes of people, or saying that certain lifestyles are wrong while affirming others as right, etc. To Rohr, avoiding those categories means "nondual." We will discuss this more in depth later in this chapter.
4 Richard Rohr and Andreas Ebert. *The Enneagram: A Christian Perspective* (New York, NY: Crossroad Publishing, 2001), pp. xvi-xviii.
5 Richard Rohr and Andreas Ebert (trans. Peter Heinegg). *Discovering the Enneagram: An Ancient Tool for a New Spiritual Journey* (New York, NY: Crossroad Publishing, 1992), p. xiii. Credit for this information goes to Dr. Ronald V. Huggins.
6 Ibid., p. xv.
7 Richard Rohr and Andreas Ebert. *The Enneagram: A Christian Perspective* (New York, NY: Crossroad Publishing, 2001), pp. xxiii.
8 Richard Rohr. *The Universal Christ* (New York, NY: Convergent Books, 2019), p. 28.
    Also see Richard Rohr. "The Universal Christ" *Center for Action and Contemplation (CAC)* website (Sun., Dec. 2, 2018) https://cac.org/who-is-christ-2018-12-02/.
9 Richard Rohr. "Christ Since the Beginning" *Center for Action and Contemplation (CAC)* website (Thurs., Feb. 21, 2019); https://cac.org/the-first-incarnation-2019-02-21/; also see video Richard Rohr. "The Cosmic Christ." *YouTube* video at 4:00-minute mark. (We also have video on file.); https://www.youtube.com/watch?v=4LYQQO5uFtA.
10 Op. cit. Rohr, *The Universal Christ*, p. 28.
11 Richard Rohr. "'Christ' is Another Word for Everything" *Center for Action and Contemplation (CAC)* website (Thurs., April 5, 2017); https://cac.org/christ-another-word-everything-2017-04-05/.
12 *"**Panentheism** sees God as both distinct from and dependent on the world at the same time. God comes from the world, and the world comes from God. It is a symbiotic relationship. Ron Brooks and Norman Geisler*

describe panentheism by saying that 'God is to the world what the soul is to the body.' God is ultimate reality (panentheism literally means "all in God"). Because our souls are our essence which, in turn are a part of the ultimate reality, we are all a part of God, though we are not God. And because the world is ever changing, God is also ever changing. As our souls learn and grow, God becomes more powerful. God then uses that power to create new things for us to learn. God is learning and growing just as we are.

"One way to envision panentheism is to view God as both a seed and a tree. The tree represents everything God could possibly become. The seed represents the actual state that God (and, consequently, the world) is now in. But in panentheism, the seed never actualizes a tree. Although God is always growing and changing, God will never attain all that is possible to become. This is why panentheism is also known as process theology— God is always in process."

D. Powell. *Holman QuickSource Guide to Christian Apologetics* (Nashville, TN: Holman Reference, 2006), p. 105.

13 *"**Pantheism** means all ('pan') is God ('theism'). It is the worldview held by most Hindus, many Buddhists, and other New Age religions. It is also the worldview of Christian Science, Unity, and Scientology.*

"According to pantheism, God 'is all in all.' God pervades all things, contains all things, subsumes all things, and is found within all things. Nothing exists apart from God; and all things are in some way identified with God. The world is God; and God is the world. But more precisely in pantheism, all is God, and God is all."

Norman L. Geisler. *Baker Encyclopedia of Christian Apologetics* (Grand Rapids, MI: Baker Books, 1999), p. 580.

14 Richard Rohr. "The Christification of the Universe," *Center for Action and Contemplation (CAC)* website (Sun., Nov. 6, 2016); https://cac.org/the-christification-of-the-universe-2016-11-06/.

15 Richard Rohr. "This Is My Body" *Center for Action and Contemplation (CAC)* website (Mon., March 4, 2019); https://cac.org/you-are-the-body-of-christ-2019-03-04/.

16 Richard Rohr. "Christ in Paul's Eyes" *Center for Action and Contemplation (CAC)* website (Wed., Feb. 27, 2019), https://cac.org/in-christ-2019-02-27/.

17 See written response to Rohr's use of these texts in Marcia Montenegro. "'Who do men say that I am?' An Evaluation of Richard Rohr's *Universal Christ*" *Christian Answers for the New Age (CANA);* (First published April 2019.); http://www.christiananswersforthenewage.org/Articles_UniversalChrist.aspx.

18 Richard Rohr. "What Do We Do With the Bible?" *Center for Action* *and Contemplation (CAC)* website (Sun., Jan. 6, 2019); https://cac.org/what-do-we-do-with-the-bible-2019-01-06/.

19 Ibid.

20 Richard Rohr. "The Bible—The Problem and the Solution: Richard Rohr" *YouTube* video (Dec. 12, 2017) with Richard Rohr; https://www.youtube.com/watch?v=UaJd1nQWAno. Rohr does not mention Wilber in this video clip, but he is referring to Wilber's system, which he does elsewhere as well, especially on his website.

See "Tag Archives: Ken Wilber" *Center for Action and Contemplation (CAC)* website; https://cac.org/tag/ken-wilber/.

Wilber teaches there are levels of consciousness (Spiral Dynamics) through which man moves upward from the primitive and instinctual to religious, rational, and others, with the eventual goal being the highest level of nondual which he adopted from someone else.

Richard Rohr. "Spiral Dynamics: Levels of Development - Week 1" *Center for Action and Contemplation (CAC)* website (Fri., Dec. 11, 2015); https://cac.org/spiral-dynamics-2015-12-11/.

21 Richard Rohr. *The Universal Christ* (New York, NY: Convergent Books, 2019), p. 27.

22 Ibid., p. 33 and 147.

23 Ibid., p. 225.

24 Ibid., p. 120.

25 Rich Heffern. "The Eternal Christ in the Cosmic Story" *National Catholic Reporter* (Dec. 11, 2009); https://www.ncronline.org/news/spirituality/eternal-christ-cosmic-story. (Accessed October 2019.)

26 Ibid.

27 Ibid.

28 Richard Rohr. "Another Name for Everything: Jesus and Christ" *Center for Action and Contemplation (CAC)* website (Tues., Feb. 12, 2019); https://cac.org/another-name-for-every-thing-2019-02-12/.

29 Op. cit. Rich Heffern.

30 Richard Rohr. "Loving Both Jesus and Christ," *Center for Action and Contemplation (CAC)* website (Fri., March 31, 2017); https://cac.org/loving-jesus-christ-2017-03-31/.

31 Richard Rohr. "The Universal Christ" *Center for Action and Contemplation (CAC)* website (Sun., Dec. 2, 2018); https://cac.org/who-is-christ-2018-12-02/.

32 Richard Rohr. *The Universal Christ* (New York, NY: Convergent Books, 2019), p. 178.

33 Richard Rohr. "Beyond Words: Wisdom's Way of Knowing" *Center for Action and Contemplation (CAC)* website (Thurs., Jan. 15, 2015); https://cac.org/beyond-words-2015-01-15/.

34 Richard Rohr. "Interfaith Friendship" *Center for Action and Contemplation (CAC)* website (Mon., Sept. 26, 2016); https://cac.org/interfaith-friendship-2016-09-26/.

35 Richard Rohr. "The Universal Christ: Another Name For Everything" *Center for Action and Contemplation (CAC)* website (2019); https://cac.org/another-name-for-every-thing-the-universal-christ/.

36 Richard Rohr. "The Perennial Tradition" *Center for Action and Contemplation (CAC)* website; https://cac.org/living-school/program-details/the-perennial-tradition/.

37 Richard Rohr. "A Change of Consciousness: Emerging Church" *Center for Action and Contemplation (CAC)* website (Wed., Nov. 29, 2017); https://cac.org/a-change-of-consciousness-2017-11-29/.

38 Richard Rohr. "Contemplation" *Center for Action and Contemplation (CAC)* website; https://cac.org/about-cac/contemplation/.

39 See Marcia Montenegro. "Contemplating Contemplative Prayer: Is It Really Prayer?" *Christian Answers for the New Age (CANA);* http://www.christiananswersforthenewage.org/Articles_ContemplativePrayer1.html.

Also see online book by Waner, Medina, Crabtree. *Silent God, Silent Man: Revealing the True Heart of the Spiritual Formation Movement* (Kansas City, MO: TheologyThinkTank, 2018; pdf online); https://theologythinktank.com/wp-content/uploads/2015/10/Silent-God-Silent-Man-Chris-Waner-and-Brandon-Medina.pdf.

40 Richard Rohr. "What is Contemplative Prayer and Why is it So Needed? with Fr. Richard Rohr" *YouTube* video (Jan. 10, 2018); http://bit.ly/2lNiHLN. (Video on file.)

Chapter 6 — Reap the Whirlwind

1 Tom Nash. "A Primer on Richard Rohr" *Catholic Answers* website; https://www.catholic.com/qa/a-primer-on-richard-rohr.

2 Meghan Lally. "Dallas' Suzanne Stabile Dedicates Her Life to Enneagram Education," *D[allas] Magazine* (August 24, 2018); https://www.dmagazine.com/health-fitness/2018/08/suzanne-stabile-enneagram/.

Zondervan promotion, "Sacred Enneagram by Renowned Enneagram Expert Chris Heuertz Sells Over 100000 Copies: New Interactive Companion Workbook to Release in November" *Zondervan* website (October 4, 2019); https://www.zondervan.com/blog/2019/10/04/sacred-enneagram-by-renowned-enneagram-expert-chris-heuertz-sells-over-100000-copies/.

3 Founders page on *Gravity: A Center for Contemplative Activism* website: https://gravitycenter.com/home-page/host/community/founders/.

4 Phileena and Chris Heuertz also appear on "Interviews—Doing Good Better: Active Contemplation in Christian Spirituality" *The Table* (Biola

University Center for Christian Thought); https://cct.biola.edu/doing-good-better-active-contemplation/.

5 This writer came across assertions of the Enneagram as ancient and Christian in every talk or podcast from a Christian Enneagram teacher or speaker and on every Christian site promoting the Enneagram.

6 Op. cit. Zondervan.

7 K. Mulhern. "Seeing the Face of God: A Patheos Q&A with Ian Morgan Cron and Suzanne Stabile" *Patheos* blog (Oct. 21, 2016); https://www.patheos.com/blogs/takeandread/2016/10/seeing-the-face-of-god-a-patheos-qa-with-ian-morgan-cron-and-suzanne-stabile/.

8 Op. cit. Megan Lally. Richard Rohr is called Stabile's "spiritual mentor."

9 For more information on Cron and Stabile, see Marcia Montenegro. "The Christian Enneagram Authors: What You Should Know and Why" *Christian Answers for the New Age (CANA)* (May 2019); http://www.christiananswersforthenewage.org/Articles_ChristianEnneagramAuthors.aspx.

10 "About" *Christian Soul Care—Inviting God's Touch into Your Soul* website; http://www.christiansoulcare.com/about/. (Accessed February 7, 2020)

11 Ibid. *"Kristi Gaultiere, Psy.D. has earned a Doctorate degree in Clinical Psychology and a Masters degree in Marriage and Family Therapy. She is a licensed Professional Counselor (LPC4), licensed Marriage and Family Therapist (#MFT29887), and certified Spiritual Director."*

12 Ibid.

13 Ibid.

14 Bill Gaultiere. "The Enneagram: Sin, Emotions, and Jesus" *YouTube* video (Oct. 13, 2017); https://www.youtube.com/watch?v=23DOQCqvsxA.

15 Ibid.

16 The *Faithlife Study Bible* comments: *"**who brought you up** - The same phrase is used in Exod 32:4 to describe the golden calf Aaron and the people made in Moses' absence. In both instances, the people viewed the calves as an acceptable means of approaching Yahweh."*

J.D. Barry, et al., "1 Ki 12:28" *Faithlife Study Bible* (Bellingham, WA; Lexham Press: 2012, 2016).

17 Op. cit. Bill Gaultiere. The comments about Jesus and Richard Rohr are in the first 13 minutes of the video.

18 Ibid. Bill Gaultiere. See at approximately 12:48 minute mark and 13:00 minute mark.

19 Pastor Paul Taylor. "What's Your Number?" *Rivers Crossing* website, (August 18, 2019); https://subsplash.com/riverscrossing/lb/mi/+wv5sq3v. Remarks made around the 9:10 and 11:30 marks. We also have the video on file. Marcia Montenegro wrote Pastor Taylor giving him information on the Enneagram, but his reply ignored the information.

20 Pastor Matt Brown. "Enneagram #1 The Reformer / Sandals Church" *YouTube* video (Apr 16, 2018); https://www.youtube.com/watch?v=_ Hyqy3BTlFI. The statements are all made in the first 5:13 minutes of the video.

21 Richard Rohr. "False Self and True Self, Part 1 - Mystics and Nondual Thinkers: Week 6" *Center for Action and Contemplation (CAC)* website (Tues., Aug. 18, 2015); https://cac.org/false-self-true-self-part-1-2015-08-18/.

22 Ibid.

23 Ibid.

24 Ibid.

25 *"This book likens True Self to a diamond, buried deep within us, formed under the intense pressure of our lives, that must be searched for, uncovered, separated from all the debris of ego that surrounds it. In a sense True Self must, like Jesus, be resurrected, and that process is not resuscitation but transformation."*

Richard Rohr *Immortal Diamond* book promo at *The Bookstore at the CAC* website; https://store.cac.org/products/immortal-diamond?_ga=2.91069267.871590903.1574714152-1171973742.1551898521.

26 Rich Heffern. "The Eternal Christ in the Cosmic Story" *National Catholic Reporter* (Dec. 11, 2009); https://www.ncronline.org/news/spirituality/eternal-christ-cosmic-story. (Accessed October 2019.)

27 Although the term "Christ Consciousness" is used in New Thought and the New Age, in those contexts it specifically means that one must achieve a state of realizing one's inherent Christ nature. Rohr does believe all have "divine DNA" and that Christ is in all, but he stops short of claiming we have an inherent Christ nature or that we are Christ.

28 Ian Morgan Cron and Suzanne Stabile. *The Road Back to You: An Enneagram Journey to Self-Discovery* (Downers Grove, IL: InterVarsity Press, 2016), p. 15 and 18.

29 Ibid., p. 24. The same quote is found on Rohr's blog, and there is credited to Rohr's book *Immortal Diamond* (which may be quoting Thomas Merton).

30 Author Page "David B. Benner, PhD." *Baker Publishing Group* website; http://bakerpublishinggroup.com/authors/david-g-benner-phd/90.

31 A search led to the revealing information that David G. Benner is a "Master Teacher" at Richard Rohr's Living School for Action and Contemplation. "Board of Reference (BOR)-Meet Our Board of Reference: David G. Benner, Ph.D." *Center Quest* website; https://www.cqcenterquest.org/about/board-of-reference/.

Also under "Editorial Reviews: About the Author" on *Amazon* website: https://amzn.to/2nu13O8.

32 *Selah Center* website: Cascadia Living Wisdom School, Gig Harbor,

Washington; https://selahcenter.org/.

33 David G. Benner. *Living Wisdom, Revised and Expanded* (Eugene, OR: Wipf and Stock Publishers, 2nd ed., Revised, Expanded edition, July 24, 2019), p. 73.

34 See chapter 5 of this book to read about Richard Rohr's beliefs about perennialism.

35 Op. cit. David G. Benner, *Living Wisdom*

36 Ibid., p. 64.

37 Ibid., p. 74.

38 Dr. David G. Benner. "Faith and Belief" *Dr. David G. Benner* website (Posted on August 5, 2016); https://web.archive.org/web/20170224150340/http://www.drdavidgbenner.ca/faith-and-belief/.

39 Dr. David G. Benner. "Wisdom" *Dr. David G. Benner* website (Posted September 30, 2016); https://web.archive.org/web/20161231080801/http://www.drdavidgbenner.ca/wisdom/.

40 "*Panentheism sees God as both distinct from and dependent on the world at the same time. God comes from the world, and the world comes from God. It is a symbiotic relationship. Ron Brooks and Norman Geisler describe Panentheism by saying that 'God is to the world what the soul is to the body.' God is ultimate reality (Panentheism literally means all in God). Because our souls are our essence which, in turn, is a part of the ultimate reality, we are all a part of God, though we are not God. And because the world is ever-changing, God is also ever-changing. As our souls learn and grow, God becomes more powerful. God then uses that power to create new things for us to learn. God is learning and growing just as we are.*

"*One way to envision Panentheism is to view God as both a seed and a tree. The tree represents everything God could possibly become. The seed represents the actual state that God (and, consequently, the world) is now in. But in Panentheism, the seed never actualizes a tree. Although God is always growing and changing, God will never attain all that is possible to become. This is why Panentheism is also known as process theology—God is always in process.*"

D. Powell. *Holman QuickSource Guide to Christian Apologetics* (Nashville, TN: Holman Reference, 2006), p. 105.

41 *Perennialism* is the belief that there is one core truth at the center of all beliefs/religions.

42 "The Rev. Dr. Cynthia Bourgeault" *The Contemplative Society* website; https://www.contemplative.org/cynthia-bourgeault/.

43 "*Those of you who have been working with Cynthia know how much the Fourth Way Gurdjieff wisdom tradition and the Teilhardian wisdom stream have influenced her thinking,*" on Bourgeault's *The Wisdom Way* *of Knowing* Wisdom School website; at https://wisdomwayofknowing. org/resource-directory/mr-gurdjieff-meet-mr-teilhard-2019-wisdom-school/.

See also, Cynthia Bourgeault. "'Whur We Come From' (letter from Cynthia);" https://wisdomwayofknowing.org/resource-directory/whur-we-come-from/.

44 Richard Rohr's endorsement on Helen Palmer's page "Richard Rohr says about Helen Palmer" *Enneagram.com* website; www.enneagram. com/helen_palmer.html.

45 DVD of talk. Richard Rohr and Russ Hudson. "Enneagram as a Tool for Spiritual Journey – DVD" *The Bookstore at the CAC* website; https:// store.cac.org/products/enneagram-as-a-tool-for-spiritual-journey-dvd.

46 Marcia Montenegro, co-author of this book, noticed the changes from the time she wrote her first article on the Enneagram in 2011 to when the Enneagram surged in the church from 2017 to the present.

47 Theodorre Donson also has written under the name of Theodore E. Dobson.

48 "History and Founders" *International Enneagram Association (IEA)* website; https://www.internationalenneagram.org/about/the-iea/history-and-founders/#!directory/ord=lnm.

49 "Maria Beesing: Common Knowledge" *Library Thing* website; https://www.librarything.com/author/beesingmaria.

50 See speakers at "The Enneagram Global Summit: 9 Essential Pathways for Transformation" *The Shift Network* website; https:// enneagramglobalsummit.com/.

51 See program booklet *"IEA 25 Foundations for the Future: Moving Forward with the Enneagram"* (pdf online); https://ieaninepoints.com/wp-content/uploads/2019/01/2019_IEA_Global_Conference_Program.pdf.

52 Adele Ahlberg Calhoun and Doug Calhoun. *Spiritual Rhythms for the Enneagram: A Handbook for Harmony and Transformation* (Downers Grove, IL: InterVarsity Press, IVP Books, March 2019).
For list of names see Marcia Montenegro. "Christian Book Thanks New Agers: IVP Book on Enneagram" *Facebook,* Christian Answers for the New Age (CANA); (September 2, 2019); http://bit.ly/2ltaxbs_

53 https://www.zondervan.com/9780310348276/the-sacred-enneagram/.

54 Suzanne Stabile describes herself as an "Enneagram Master" on her site at http://bit.ly/35C4svZ.

55 "Meet Beth McCord" at McCord's *Your Enneagram Coach* website; https://www.yourenneagramcoach.com/yec-about-beth.

56 Ibid., under "Credentials."

57 Dr. A. J. Sherrill. "Dr. AJ Sherrill – Lenten Enneagram" *vimeo* video (March 5, 2019); https://vimeo.com/ondemand/lentenenneagram;

Bill Gaultiere. "The Enneagram: Sin, Emotions, and Jesus" *YouTube* video (Oct. 13, 2017); https://www.youtube.com/watch?v=23DOQCqvsxA;

Pastor Paul Taylor. "What's Your Number?" *Rivers Crossing* website, (August 18, 2019); https://subsplash.com/riverscrossing/lb/mi/+wv5sq3v;

Pastor Matt Brown of Sandals Church in California gave a series of sermons on the Enneagram. "Enneagram #1 The Reformer / Sandals Church" *YouTube* video (Apr 16, 2018); https://www.youtube.com/watch?v=_Hyqy3BTlFI.

Chapter 7 — As For This Moses . . .

1 Wayne Grudem. *Bible Doctrine* (Grand Rapids, MI: Zondervan, 1999), p. 86.

2 G.D. Fee and R.L. Hubbard, (Eds.). *The Eerdmans Companion to the Bible* (Grand Rapids, MI; Cambridge, U.K.: William B. Eerdmans Publishing Company, 2011), p. 120.

3 Allegra Hobbs. "The Self-Help Movement That Is Upending American Christianity," *Forge* (November 26, 2019); https://forge.medium.com/the-self-help-movement-that-is-upending-american-christianity-9ce381e10d4f. (Copy on file.)

4 Christian Smith and Melinda Lundquist Denton. *Soul Searching: The Religious and Spiritual Lives of American Teenagers* (New York, NY: Oxford University Press, 2005), pp. 162–163.

5 Kenneth Berding. "The Not-So-Sacred Enneagram: A Book Review of 'The Sacred Enneagram' by Christopher L. Heuertz", *The Good Book Blog: Talbot School of Theology* (November 15, 2018); https://www.biola.edu/blogs/good-book-blog/2018/the-not-so-sacred-enneagram.

6 Jonathan Merritt. "What is the 'Enneagram,' and why are Christians suddenly so enamored by it," *Religious News Service* (September 5, 2017); https://religionnews.com/2017/09/05/what-is-the-enneagram-and-why-are-christians-suddenly-so-enamored-by-it/.

7 Bob Smietana. "Americans Love God and the Bible, Are Fuzzy on the Details" *LifeWay Research* (September 27, 2016); https://lifewayresearch.com/2016/09/27/americans-love-god-and-the-bible-are-fuzzy-on-the-details/.

8 "Survey Finds Most American Christians Are Actually Heretics", G. Shane Morris; https://thefederalist.com/2016/10/10/survey-finds-american-christians-actually-heretics/

9 Sarajane Case, *Instagram* bio; https://www.instagram.com/sarajanecase/.

10 Op. cit. Allegra Hobbs.

11 Christopher L.Heuertz. *The Sacred Enneagram* (Grand Rapids, MI: Zondervan Publishing, 2017), Kindle Edition, p. 29.
12 Ibid., p. 72.
13 For a fuller treatment, see: "Pelagianism" *Theopedia*; https://www.theopedia.com/pelagianism.
14 Op. cit. Allegra Hobbs.

Chapter 8 — One Last Question: Can God Redeem Anything?
1 "Beth McCord/Your Enneagram Coach" *Family Christian* website; https://familychristian.com/contributors/beth-mccord-your-enneagram-coach. (Accessed January 7, 2020.)
2 Ibid.
3 Misty Phillip. "Episode 49: Marriage and the Enneagram: Beth & Jeff McCord" *By His Grace* podcast (January 14, 2020); https://mistyphillip.com/marriage-and-the-enneagram-beth-jeff-mccord/. (Accessed January 7, 2020)
4 See Marcia Montenegro. "Bringing Up the Dead: The Case of Saul and the Medium" *Facebook,* Christian Answers for the New Age (CANA); (October 25, 2019); https://www.facebook.com/103502882236/posts/10156263721122237/.
5 Mitch Pacwa, SJ. *Catholics and the New Age: How Good People Are Being Drawn into Jungian Psychology, the Enneagram, and the Age of Aquarius* (Ann Arbor, MI: Servant Publications, 1992), p.116.
6 Ibid., p. 117.
7 *"**Psychometrics** is a field of study concerned with the theory and technique of psychological measurement. As defined by the US National Council on Measurement in Education (NCME), psychometrics refers to psychological measurement. Generally, it refers to the field in psychology and education that is devoted to testing, measurement, assessment, and related activities."* "Psychometrics" *Wikipedia, The Free Encyclopedia;* https://en.wikipedia.org/wiki/Psychometrics.
8 Jay Medenwaldt. "The Enneagram, Science, and Christianity - Part 1" *Jay Medenwaldt* website (Tuesday, January 15, 2019); http://www.jaymedenwaldt.com/2019/01/the-enneagram-science-and-christianity.html. (Accessed February 7, 2020.)
9 Additional suggested reading:
   Marcia Montenegro. "What About the Enneagram?" *Southern Evangelical Seminary blog* (November 4); https://ses.edu/what-about-the-enneagram/.
   Marcia Montenegro. "The Genetic Fallacy, Exceptions, and the Enneagram" *Facebook,* Christian Answers for the New Age (CANA); (January 31); https://www.facebook.com/103502882236/posts/10156513695947237/.

Scripture Index

Ministry Resources

Christian Answers for the New Age (CANA)
P.O. Box 7191
Arlington, VA 22207-0191
Marcia Montenegro, Founder and Director
Website: www.christiananswersforthenewage.org
Facebook: Christian Answers for the New Age

Midwest Christian Outreach, Inc. (MCOI)
P.O. Box 446
Wonder Lake, IL 60097-0446
Phone: 630-627-9028
Website: www.midwestoutreach.org
Facebook: Midwest Christian Outreach Inc.
Email: info@midwestoutreach.org
YouTube: www.youtube.com/c/MidwestoutreachOrg

Watchman Fellowship, Inc.
PO Box 13340
Arlington, TX 76094- 0340
Phone: 817-277-0023
Website: www.watchman.org

Probe Ministries
2001 W. Plano Parkway, Suite 2000
Plano, TX 75075-8610
Phone: 972-941-4565
Website: www.probe.org

Doreen Virtue
Contact: Instagram.com/DoreenVirtue direct messages
Website: DoreenVirtue.com
Facebook: DoreenVirtueForJesus
YouTube: DoreenVirtueForJesus

About the Authors

Don & Joy Veinot

L.L. (Don) and Joy Veinot are co-founders and he is president of Midwest Christian Outreach, Inc. (MCOI), a mission to cults and non-Christian religions based in Wonder Lake, IL. Don and Joy (his wife since 1970) have been involved in discernment ministry as missionaries to New Religious Movements since 1987.

Don is a frequent guest on numerous radio and television broadcasts including *The John Ankerberg Show* as well as being a staff researcher and writer for the *Midwest Christian Outreach, Inc. Journal*. Additionally, Don is co-author of the book *A Matter of Basic Principles: Bill Gothard and the Christian Life* as well as contributing author of *Preserving Evangelical Unity: Welcoming Diversity in Non-Essentials*. Furthermore, he is the author of various research articles in the *CRI Journal, PFO Quarterly Journal, Campus Life Magazine, Journal of the International Society of Christian Apologetics, Midwestern Journal of Theology,* and other periodicals.

Don was ordained to the ministry by West Suburban Community Church of Lombard, IL at the Garden of Gethsemane in Jerusalem, Israel in March of 1997. He is a charter member of International Society of Christian Apologetics (ISCA) and is also the current President of Evangelical Ministries to New Religions (EMNR), a consortium of counter-cult/apologetic and discernment ministries from around the country. In addition, Don co-hosts a weekly webcast with Ron Henzel, Senior Researcher for MCOI, called *"The Unknown Webcast,"* which can be found on their YouTube channel at www.youtube.com/c/MidwestoutreachOrg.

The MCOI website is www.midwestoutreach.org. MCOI also has a weekly e-letter, *The Crux,* and you can follow Midwest Christian Outreach, Inc. on *Facebook, Twitter, LinkedIn, Parler,* and *USA.Life*.

Marcia Montenegro

Before becoming a Christian, Marcia Montenegro was involved for many years in Eastern spiritual beliefs (Hindu and Buddhist), New Age, and occult practices. She was also a certified, professional astrologer who taught astrology for several years and served as chairperson of the Astrology Board of Examiners (ABE) and President of the Astrological Society in Atlanta, GA. Through her full-time ministry, Christian Answers for the New Age (CANA), Marcia speaks around the country at churches and conferences and on numerous radio broadcasts, internet webcasts, and podcasts. She has articles published in various magazines and written chapters included in books on the New Age and occult topics.

Marcia has a Master's Degree in Religion from Southern Evangelical Seminary, Charlotte, NC. Marcia serves as a missionary with Fellowship International Mission (FIM), Allentown, PA. Based in Arlington, VA, she is the mother of an adult son and also the author of *SpellBound: The Paranormal Seduction of Today's Kids* (Cook, 2006).

Marcia's CANA website is www.christiananswersforthenewage. org. You can also follow her on Facebook at Christian Answers for the New Age.